Letters To My Teenage Self Volume Two

Camila Piombini, Amanda Wilson, Louise Plunkett, Janice Watson, Michele Dickerson, Param Kaur-Kingston, Marta Suchomska, Racheal Beattie, Vie Portland, Cassie Swift, Nicole Bateman, Danielle Maynard

Print ISBN: 978-1-7391545-2-3

1st Edition

Some names and identifying details have been changed to protect the privacy of individuals

Disclaimer: The opinions and information expressed in this publication are those of the authors only and do not represent professional advice. This book is not intended a substitute for seeking professional medical advice and the reader should regularly consult a medical expert in matters relating to his/her health, and particularly with respect to any symptoms that might require diagnosis or medical attention. The authors take no responsibility for any actions taken as a result of reading this book, and do not assume and hereby disclaim any liability for any losses occurring as a result.

Contents

Foreword

By Nicole Bateman

I am excited to introduce you to Letters to My Teenage Self Volume Two. This book is a collection of heartfelt letters from amazing authors who know exactly what it's like to be a teenager. They've come together to share their stories, offer advice, and let you know that you are never alone in your journey.

You see, being a teenager can be tough. We all go through ups and downs, face challenges, and sometimes question who we are and where we're going. But guess what? These incredible authors have been there too, and they've come out stronger and wiser on the other side. They want you to know that you have the power to overcome anything that comes your way.

In this book, you'll discover a treasure trove of wisdom and encouragement. The authors tackle all sorts of topics that matter to teenagers like you—making friends, embracing your true self, dealing with mental health and so much more. They pour their hearts out on these pages, sharing their experiences, lessons learned, and the invaluable advice they wish they had received as teenagers.

Let me tell you, these letters are like rays of sunshine on a cloudy day. They're here to lift you up, remind you of your worth, and inspire you to embrace all the beautiful possibilities that lie ahead. Each letter is like a warm hug from someone who truly understands what you're going through. You'll find comfort in their stories, find strength in their resilience, and find hope in their triumphs.

If you're a teenager reading this, know that you are not alone. You have a whole community of authors and readers cheering you on. You are stronger than you think, and your goals are worth chasing. Embrace the guidance, soak in the stories, and let them fuel your belief in yourself.

And to the parents and guardians out there, this book is for you too. It offers a glimpse into the hearts and minds of teenagers, helping you understand the challenges they face and how to support them on this wild rollercoaster ride called adolescence.

I want to express my heartfelt gratitude to the incredible authors who have poured their souls into Letters to My Teenage Self Volume Two. Your bravery, compassion, and generosity will touch the lives of so many young readers, offering them a helping hand when they need it most.

So, my friend, get ready to embark on an amazing journey. Letters to My Teenage Self Volume Two is here to uplift, inspire, and remind you that you are never alone. Let these letters be your companions, your confidants, and your guides as you navigate the incredible adventure of being a teenager.

With love,

Nicole

Best-selling author of 'My Child Has Exams...Now What?' and 'Letters to My Teenage Self', curator of this book collaboration, owner of A Box Full of Joy and co-founder of The Super Sensory Squad

Chapter One

To the teen who is known as 'the quiet one'

by Danielle Maynard

To the teen who is known as 'the quiet one',

"Is she always this quiet?"

"Is she ok?"

"Does she speak?"

"Oh, you know what they say, the quiet ones are the worst ones."

This is what I grew up hearing time and time again. I hated the label of being shy. I remember feeling like something was wrong with me. Why did everyone keep pointing this out to me? Was I weird?

Have you heard any of the above? If yes, then don't worry you're not alone. That's why I am writing this for you. I am writing this to let you know that it's ok to stay in the background it's okay to not always have something to say it's ok that you might need time to sit back and observe your surroundings. Most importantly, to tell you that you will find your voice in your own time, in your own way and others will see you, understand you and appreciate you.

It all started at a young age really, I was brought up with a fair few loud characters in my family. From the outside I probably stuck out like a sore thumb. But what people didn't know is that hearing those statements actually made me feel insecure, and self-critical and it impacted my confidence greatly. I also felt as if I was hiding something or being manipulative. But guess what? I wasn't. I was just being ME. I wasn't being rude or conniving. I just needed a bit of time to warm up to people. I liked to sit back and enjoy my environment and observe and take things in. Not to mention that a few things happened to me at the tender age of eight that probably played a part in making me who I am.

I mean how does an eight year old who just lost her dad in a tragic car accident deal with that? Then include having to welcome a new step-dad and step-siblings into the home.

Moving to another city and leaving all your school friends, plus starting a new school all in one year. That's a lot to deal with wouldn't you say? Maybe this contributed to me being less vocal than others and feeling a tad withdrawn. What happens in your early childhood tends to follow you through your life, especially if it's not spoken about. This is why it's so important for you to find the one person with whom you can speak and share your feelings. This doesn't have to be your parents. It can be a trusted friend, relative or someone in your school perhaps.

So, let's talk about school. I don't really remember my so-called shyness being an issue in primary school as such. I would say it was more around family and once starting secondary school that it became an issue. I remember my first day at secondary school in the massive hall that was filled with a mountain of noise, voices from everywhere, faces everywhere. I felt helpless and I remember going to sit right at the back of the room. I vaguely remember seeing lots of different groups of girls and boys all huddling together having a chat. Inside I was dying to go and sit with them, but my body wouldn't allow me to. All of these thoughts would come into my head. What if they tell me to go away, what if they just ignore me? So many what ifs.

I imagine that I was not the only person feeling like that. But what made it difficult to me was the constant reminders of being shy and quiet from everyone else which most likely heightened my anxiety. Time went on in school and I slowly grew my circle of friends, but still within my own circle I was still always known as the 'quiet one'. What did this mean to me? It meant I did things that I didn't necessarily want to do just so I could fit in somehow, or for me to appear louder than I actually was, such as smoking and being cheeky in the classroom.

English was my worst lesson, as we often had to read things out loud in class, which I hated! I remember hoping and praying that the teacher wouldn't call on me or ask me anything. That feeling of dread would come over me, my heart would start beating so fast and I wanted to curl up in a big ball and the ground to swallow me up. It was so bad that I would often wag (another word for purposely not going to the lesson). Not great but that's how much of an impact it had on me.

It also meant that I often wouldn't stick up for myself. I always tended to not share how I was feeling and just agree to everything, even though deep down I didn't really want to. It was almost like I had lost my voice, like nothing would come out and I would freeze, but inside I was screaming to speak. The only thing that would come out would be "ok then" or "yes I will do it". You could say I was being taken advantage of, but whose fault was that? After all, I was old enough to make my own decisions and choices, right? But sometimes my brain didn't allow that to happen. I remember feeling like a pushover and grew to the fact that everyone purposely asked me to do things for them that I didn't necessarily want to do.

I will never forget a conversation I had with a relative who told me that she would dread me coming around her house, because she knew that I would be hard work (in terms of starting and building a conversation). Was I really that bad? I asked myself. It got me thinking about what everyone else thought of me too. Did people think I was being rude, or boring? Did no one want to be around me? As you can imagine this knocked my confidence further.

Social family gatherings were the worst. Imagine being in a room full of large and wonderful characters drowning in the noise. Thinking: shall I say something? Will they hear me? Will they even be interested in what I am saying? Thinking about everyone watching me and waiting for me to say something, people commenting to my mum saying: "is she ok?" Like really could I not just be quiet, happy, and humble without it being an issue?

I guess not.

There were times when I would feel OK then bam, someone would say that dreaded sentence "Oh yes, the quiet ones are the worst ones!" That one sentence really got to me. Did they know something that I didn't know about me? What made me worse than anyone else? I was just a normal teenager who didn't have much to say, but I was made to feel like I was up to no good, or I had his master plan of hatching something terrible.

The more negative things you hear, the more you are likely to believe what is being said about you is in fact true. This is where you start to question your own character and personality, and who you are as a person. This is the damaging part, as this can lead you to change the way you are as a person or push you to do things just to fit in and to please people. This is wrong and you shouldn't feel this way. You only need to look deep within yourself and embrace everything about you (including your flaws - because let's face it we are not made to be perfect), embrace your strengths, your character, your weirdness, and love everything that makes you, you.

Remember you won't be liked by everyone and that's fine. You won't be able to please everyone and that's fine too. As long as you stay true to yourself, that's all that matters.

Focus and surround yourself with the people that do like you and who understand you. Be around people that will support and love you for who you are, whether you're the loudest in the room or the quietest mouse on the street. Why? Because you shouldn't be made to feel different, or the odd one out, because you're not loud or as outspoken as others. I get It's easy to feel lost in a room full of noise. But remember that you are not on your own. There are many others that feel the way you do too. You will learn how to navigate this as you get older but try not to keep things in. Let people know how you are feeling and get the conversation started. Don't overthink things and everything will come out at the right time.

To this day when I am in groups the thought of 'right I better say something quick' runs through my mind, but as an adult, I can now overlook this and naturally, I just wait to speak when I am ready. It's something that I can now deal with and live with. I speak when I feel comfortable too. I spark conversations with no problem, sometimes before anyone else. I can speak up for myself and share my opinions with ease. I can recognise when someone acts the way I did as a child, and guess what? I can give them that reassurance too. I guess this all takes time, and you will get there.

When you come across someone who questions your character, switch it around and tell them how you feel. You might just get them to think about how they have made you feel and in turn, make them look at themselves. This could have a lasting impact on them and others too.

Remember you are you for a reason, and no one can take that away from you.

About Author

Danielle Maynard

Danielle is a mum of a 17-year girl who is her pride and joy. Danielle loves and has worked with children and families for the past 8+ years and currently practises as a specialist nurse for children in care for the NHS. Danielle was not very confident as a child and was very shy and knew that she wanted to do something for girls who might be feeling just like her. As a result, Danielle created her business Serenity for Girls.

Serenity for Girls aims to empower pre-teen girls and to help girls to gain more confidence in a fun and positive way. Danielle has a dream of starting her very own girls club where she can continue to help young girls navigate through the adolescence period with beams of confidence and lots of smiles.

www.serenityforgirls.co.uk

www.instagram.com/serenityforgirls

Chapter Two

To the teen who feels they have no worth

By Vie Portland

To the teen who feels they have no worth,

Gorgeous girl. I can feel you wincing already, believing I couldn't possibly be talking to you. I know you have an urge to look over your shoulder, to see if I'm talking to someone standing behind you.

I'm not. I'm talking to you, to the me that was. I'm going to tell you that things will not always be the way they are for you now; that there will come a time in your life when you believe what people say about you: that you are beautiful both inside and outside; that you have made a difference; that you have changed their lives.

Are you wanting to look over your shoulder again? You don't believe that any of these wonderful things could be said about you, do you?

I remember that feeling so well. It was my constant companion for years, decades. I used to describe all the pain I felt as an iron rugby ball living in the pit of my stomach. It was so heavy, so uncomfortable, but I couldn't give it away because I only knew how to live with it. It was the only thing that felt like mine. I disliked myself so much that I also felt like I deserved the pain too.

I remember feeling that love wasn't good, yet I craved it. The people that said they loved me hurt me over and over again, from as young as I could recall. If that was love, I couldn't live with any more of it. But oh, darling girl, I know you desperately want the love you read about in books you find respite in. I know you want to feel loved by family, and friends. I know you long to be loved by someone who you don't have to share with family and friends too. Someone that feels like they are just yours. I also know you don't feel you will ever get it because you don't deserve it.

Present day me wants to hug you so much! I want to hold you and love you and give you a glimpse of the wonders to come, because you do deserve it. You deserve it all. And this will be a surprise, but the best love, the most rewarding, the most consistent, will be from you. It will be from the work you do to learn to love yourself. I'm laughing now, thinking of the face I would have pulled at the utter ridiculousness of such a stupid statement, but it's true! I promise you. One day, you'll decide that the time has come to make the life you want to live, to be happy. Then you'll make the same choice the next day, and the next day, and the next. Because it is a choice. It's not always an easy choice, because other things - like the things you're living with now, will come up and continue to hurt you, and unsettle you. But please, please believe me when I say they won't always feel like the biggest parts of you. One day you will realise how wonderful you are, as you are. With practice (I never said it would be easy but, goodness! It's completely worth it!), that will be how you feel about yourself nearly all of the time. I promise.

But, can I ask you to do something for me? Can I ask you to not wait as long as I did? Can I ask you to make the choice now? Can I ask you to start seeing yourself with love now?

You still don't believe me, I know. How could someone like us possibly deserve good things?

I remember how my family's words would cut me. How them telling me how fat, ugly and worthless I was, seeped right to the very core of me. Feeling that if I were cut like a tree, my rings would just say FatUglyWorthless FatUglyWorthless round and round.

I remember how it felt to feel like I could never do anything right. When I did well at school, I was a girly-swot and pathetic. At Christmas, when the extended family came together and we would play board games, how people would want to be on my team because "she thinks she's clever". But when I got questions wrong it was: "you're not as smart as you think you are." If I did things well, I was a show off. If I didn't do well then, I deserved it for having 'ideas above my station' (a silly term meaning that someone like me shouldn't wish for, or expect, better).

I tried so hard to be a 'good girl', to please everyone, to do everything right but I couldn't. I thought it was my fault. The people that love me would only tell me the truth, wouldn't they? If they were telling me these things, it must be because

I was those things. I was wrong. I was broken. I was stupid. It must be true, they told me so.

When people outside of my family told me good things, I thought they were lying, or that they were just being nice, or they thought I was pathetic, so they would throw me crumbs of pity. I craved the niceness but also felt embarrassed about it. I would think that they obviously don't know the real me, otherwise they wouldn't say those things. So, I felt guilty, collecting the compliments as if I were a thief stealing things from a shop, because I didn't deserve them as I really was.

The guilt! Goodness! I sometimes felt I was glued together with guilt. That if I didn't suffer for everything that went wrong, for myself and others, even people I had never met, I would fall apart and there would be more of me to kick around. I loved being alone: in my bedroom, engrossed in a book, or dancing around, but then I would be moaned at for thinking I was too good to spend time with the family. Guilt. Then, when I spent time with the family, I would be told I ruined things because I talked too much, or too little. Guilt. If I wanted nice things, I needed to get a job because they didn't have money to spend on me. Guilt. I got a job and would buy them things but then I was told I was deliberately making them feel bad, because I had money and they didn't. Guilt. If I got ill and needed looking after, I was told I was taking up too much of their time. Guilt. If I went to see friends, I would be told I thought I was too good for my family and I should spend more time at home. Guilt. When I was at home, I was told I got in the way. Guilt.

Guilt. Guilt. Guilt.

But you, darling one, you don't need to feel guilty. The world is not the way it is because of you. Your family is not the way it is because of you. The decisions others make are their choice, not yours, and if they blame you, they are choosing to do that rather than deal with their own emotions and actions. As you get older, this will become more apparent. Many people find it far easier to be sad, to be cruel, to criticise, than think about their own thoughts and actions. You'll find that people talk about wanting to go from caterpillar to butterfly but really, that metamorphosis is painful, sticky and smelly, so it's easier to stay as the caterpillar and attack those that become butterflies.

But you... you are on your way to being an incredible butterfly! The metamorphosis will be hard, incredibly hard, but you'll go through it and emerge gloriously! That seems impossible to you now, I know. How could someone like you ever go from a fat, ugly, worthless, gooey mess to flying high and vibrantly? It took me a long time, and I doubted it for years (I really hope you start your metamorphosis sooner than I did), with extreme lows that were brutal to get through, but I did it. And I'm so glad I did. I know you can do it too, as difficult as it seems, as difficult as it is, because you deserve to be every bit the butterfly.

I'm still a work in progress, and that's a wonderful thing! Know now, as you are in this moment, that life is full of wonder and joy, things to learn and places to see. You can be part of everything you choose to be. Never stop learning. Never stop growing. Those that stop remain as caterpillars.

Are you thinking that I'm talking nonsense? That I can't possibly be talking about you? I remember that feeling far too well. The feeling I wouldn't ever be good enough, that I would never be happy, that I didn't deserve to be happy. I lived that way for a long time.

But I can tell you that you do deserve to be happy, right now. I can tell you that you do deserve to feel love and be loved, by good people that value you. I can tell you that everything you are going through, everything you have gone through, will teach you so much about yourself, you will use everything you learn to make the lives of those you meet better too. You, gorgeous girl, really are going to be changing the world, one person at a time, because of who you are.

Why? Because you are wonderful. You are good. You are kind. You are loving. You are intelligent. You are resourceful. You are resilient. And you are loved.

Now, please make that choice to be happy. Make it now. Find the things that bring you joy. Find the people that value you. And believe it when people tell you how brilliant you are, because you are. Make the choice. Say it: I choose happiness. I choose kindness. I choose love. I choose me!

I believe in you.

Love from me, to you as you were. Love now, to you as you are. And love to you as you will be in the future.

Love always,

Vie

xx

About Author

Vie Portland

Vie Portland is many wonderful things. She is founder and director of VieNess Discover You Love You CIC, a community interest company that teaches self-esteem and confidence to children, young people, and women, as she believes everyone deserves to be happy. She is the creator of happiness products, which enable people to grow wherever they are.

She is an author of inclusive children's picture books, because she believes we all have a right to be seen, to be represented, including people with disabilities, by those who live with disabilities, as Vie does.

She is an author of Positive Growth books for adults, because she believes that it's never too late to make the choice to live your best life, and that our stories are important to share. She is a motivational speaker, because she believes, she knows, that her story helps others, and that we all deserve to have our voices heard. She is a devoted cat mum, a loving partner, a great friend. And she is happy.

https://www.vieness.co.uk

https://www.facebook.com/VieNessCIC

https://www.instagram.com/VieNessCIC

https://www.linked.com/in/VieNessCIC

https://www.youtube.com/@VieNessCIC

https://www.pinterest.co.uk/VieNessCIC

Chapter Three

To the teen who is struggling with body confidence

By Amanda Wilson

To the teen who is struggling with body confidence,

Why me? I found myself asking that question every day for most of my teenage life. Why can't I just be like the other girls in my year? I just want to have a normal body with some curves and boobs! Why can't my peers accept me for who I am, not what I look like?

You see, I was different; I was skinny, I was a late developer and was most certainly at the end of the line when boobs were handed out.

Looking back, most folk my age now would have dreamed of having a body like I had, a skinny size six that plummeted to a four with no worries about squeezing into that pair of skinny jeans, or showing off that tiny waist, but believe me I was screaming out to be that wee bit bigger.

Day in and day out I went through the same comments, stares and was made fun of. I couldn't have been at high school at a worse time. There was the Ethiopian crisis, and it was constantly on the news. I would hear: "look at her, she's come from Ethiopia, she needs to go back there, she'll be full up on a grain of rice", "do you think she has scabies?" Of course, I didn't, but the hurtful comments, the looks and stares went on and on and on.

I remember one day sitting in maths class and one of the boys thought it would be funny to see if I had a bra on and pulled my strap. I popped my head down and just got on with my work doing my best to ignore them. All the shouts of "she's filled it with her dad's socks", the laughs, the whispers just made me want to run. The teacher did his best to tell them to be quiet but somehow had lost all control of the situation. I remember thinking 'why oh why can they not pick on the girl that is overweight and leave me alone for a change'. With that thought came the feelings of guilt. We are all different shapes and sizes, and no one should be getting ridiculed just for what they look like, no matter what their shape is or the colour of their skin.

As time went on it became normal to me, I dreaded going to school. PE was my worst subject, standing in the changing room you were exposed to the girls around you. We had to take showers and I just wanted to hide away. I used to try and get into the corner of the room and get dressed as quickly as possible to hide the bones sticking through my delicate skin. In the run up to Christmas time it was especially hard as the girls had to line up on one side of the PE hall with the boys on the other, then the boys picked their partners to learn ceilidh dancing for the annual Christmas dance. I was always left until last as no one wanted to dance with me. Why, what is wrong with me? When it came to the dance 'Strip the Willow' everyone laughed trying to throw me around the room, as I just had no weight on me to keep my feet on the floor. As for swimming, don't even go there. I absolutely hated it and used every excuse under the sun to get out of those lessons. That is my big regret in life now, as I still can't swim. The memories of standing like a frozen stick at the side of the 'fish tank', as we aptly named the pool, just come flooding back.

No matter how much I ate, I just couldn't put that weight on. I was born a tiny 5lbs and I guess I was never destined to be big. I always took a packed lunch to school so I could control what I ate. Whatever I didn't eat I threw away in the bin so my parents wouldn't realise what I had eaten that day. Eating in large crowds filled me with dread, and even now, if a large plate of food is placed in front of me, I still get those butterflies. But I can have more control over my anxiety and speak out and request a small amount. I can always add to my plate when I am finished.

Not only was I ashamed of how I looked, but I had also lost all confidence in myself! I was feeling tired all the time with the constant worry, and I was a massive overthinker. I would worry about things happening at school, not only on a particular day but in the future too, when there really was nothing to worry about.

At primary school I had no problems, and I loved every minute of my school days there. I was full of energy and joined in with everything. Yes, PE wasn't my thing, but I got on and did it and gave it my best shot. Everyone played and talked with you no matter what you looked like. How could secondary not be the same? I seemed to be lost in a crowd, with no confidence or energy left in my body to stand up to the bullies. I longed to be part of a larger group of friends, as I felt that that was the place to get on in life. I have now, of course, realised this is not the case.

The more you get put down, the more you feel that nobody wants to be seen with you. I had to do something to escape and make myself feel free again, in the hope that I would get back to those happy days during the first twelve years of my life.

So, one day I thought: 'what if I make myself ill then I don't have to go to school?' Monday morning came and I just couldn't face another day of name calling, stares, giggles, and whispers behind my back. My mum was a stay-at-home parent and let us have the day off if we were ever ill. She was one of those mums that made up a bed on the sofa and brought you drinks and let you rest all day. A win-win situation, I would escape the stress of school and let my exhausted mind recover.

Sadly though, my mum also suffered from bipolar disorder and at times was admitted to hospital, so she wasn't always around. I felt, at times, I just couldn't tell her how I was feeling to add more anxiety and stress to her, so I kept all my feelings bottled up.

But today was the day. Mum was busy pottering away in the kitchen preparing breakfast, my sister was getting ready for primary school and Dad was at work, so I knew that my plan would work without getting my mum upset and stressed out. I got up, ate my breakfast very slowly then the thought of going to school just made me feel sick. That was it, go and be sick whilst the nerves and anxiety kicked in, then no way could I go in today.

I took myself off to the bathroom, locked the door and made myself sick, popping my shaking hand down my throat. Nothing happened except retching sounds, then eventually all my breakfast came back up. My stomach felt like it had been punched and kicked from all angles, but I had been sick. My plan was beginning to work. Mum asked me to unlock the door and said in her ever-soothing voice, "oh no. No school for you today, I'll make you up a bed on the sofa". Oh my gosh my plan really worked! The bus had gone, and as my mum couldn't drive there was no way she could take me down later. I remember thinking: 'I don't have to face them today!' The instant feeling of relief that came over me was amazing. Even though my tummy was sore from all the retching I had done, I felt on top of the world. Now to keep this show up, I just couldn't tell my parents how I felt or why I had made myself sick.

As the weeks passed, I somehow found the strength to go back to school, but then all the feelings of anxiety came over me again, and I felt that I just couldn't cope. I felt everyone was staring at me, laughing at me, speaking about me and I just needed a way out. So once again I played the sick card. It got harder though. Dad was getting angry and couldn't believe that I was off again. Many arguments were held between him and mum, and I felt so guilty as I had caused it. Peers at school would begin to ask questions too "Why were you off again? What is wrong with you? Is there a problem at school?" I couldn't open up to them as I felt that there was no help out there. I was also getting really tired too, of all the lying and pretending, not to mention sticking my hands down my throat and making myself sick. Little did I know at that time I was just adding to the problem. Of course, you're not going to put weight on if you are constantly worrying or throwing upmost of the time. I also had the added feeling of guilt that I wasn't helping mum with her illness. I was just adding more stress onto her and dad as they just couldn't understand what was going on.

There was nothing on my report cards from school to suggest I was struggling. In fact, I was always getting told that I worked away quietly and was a delight to have in the classroom. When everything came to light nobody could believe what I had managed to keep bottled up for many years. The lies just couldn't go on.

One day it just got so bad I let it all out. I was broken and needed help, so I told my parents everything, how I felt, the name calling, the pointing, the lack of confidence, and not having many friends. I just had to cry it all out. I was very lucky that my guidance teacher was a lovely lady and had noticed I hadn't been myself. Of course, my attendance record wasn't the greatest either, so she came out to the house and talked with me and my parents. Thank goodness it wasn't in school, as I felt I could be me in my own surroundings with loving parents around me. She got specialists[1] in to help me work on my confidence and to get back on track with my studies. I got good grades in my exams and decided to stay on and do fifth year. However, it did get a bit too much, so I dropped out of school and decided to get a job instead. I needed to get away and just restart life again.

So, at sixteen and a half I left my home, the village I grew up in, and started afresh in my new job as a general assistant in a hotel. I got to livein the staff quarters and my fellow housemates were so funny. No one called me names, no one stared when we had our meals together in the staffroom. I felt included. We had many nights of fun and laughter and at long last I was being me!I was finally getting the respect I had craved and longed for.I did get terribly homesick, but I went home on my days off. I didn't go out muchthough for fear of bumping into ex-school peers and being brought back down again. I was in such a better place, and no one was dragging me down again, so I kept myself to myself when I went home.

A couple of years passed, and I met my now husband. At the age of eighteen he didn't care what I looked like and how fat or thin I was. He loved me for who I was, and I loved him for his kind and witty personality. Oh, how he made me feel loved and alive again. He always made me laugh and was so understanding. My confidence soared and within three months of dating, he asked me to marry him. I couldn't believe it, sticking out bones, being quiet and shy, he didn't care. He wanted to spend the rest of his life with me. Yes, me! That skinny young woman that he was proud to show off to his friends and say: "she's going to spend the rest of my life with me, isn't she wonderful!"

We are still together and as for this tiny skinny body; it has given birth to four wonderful children. Remember those non-existent boobs back at the beginning of my story? They have never been big, but they have managed to feed my babies and give them the best start in life. I look at my children and I just feel accomplished. I grew them, I gave birth to them and all from my body.

I also have a lovely circle of friends who compliment me on how I look even on the days when I hang out in my pj's, and my hair is in a messy bun. They are so positive and yes, they do come in all sizes, but we embrace each other and have made lots of happy memories. When the negative thoughts come back into my head though, I just remind myself of a quote I once read in a book "shut that duck up " It's not me that has the problem with what I look like, it's others and they are usually fighting a personal issue themselves.

So, it doesn't matter what size you are, you can achieve wonderful things in life. Just remember everyone is different and if we were all the same the world would be a boring place to live. Embrace people for who they are under the skin, love them as you would love yourself. There will be times where you do feel alone and just have no energy to reach out but go and talk with your guidance teacher or year head. Talk it over with your parents too if you can. You will feel so much better. Write down your thoughts and keep a journal. Kick the negative nelly's out of your life. It's so important to have a small circle of friends that you can trust and that can help each other rather than being in a large group that don't really care or look out for each other.

Remember you are unique.

You are loved, and you are you, no matter what shape or size you are.

With lots of love, Amanda x

About Author

Amanda Wilson

Amanda is mum to four children and granny to one. She has been married to Kevin for 28 years after meeting him when she was 18. She has a passion to help others open up about their mental health struggles through the love of crafting.

Following her own struggles throughout the years, of which she is very open about, she encourages others to share their story too when the time is right for them so they can understand "It's okay to be not okay".

She has a small crafting business up in the North East of Scotland and has recently started to host workshops to help others take that time out for them and create something unique and beautiful to them through a range of mediums.

It is her mission to spread the word about how important it is to look after your mental health and that no matter what you come through in life if you work at it, you will get there and shine bright.

https://www.facebook.com/CherryGrove4

https://www.instagram/cherrygrove_bitsandbobs

https://www.linkedin.com/in/amanda-wilson-6448a0208

Chapter Four

To the teen who doesn't feel good enough

by Nicole Bateman

To the teen who doesn't feel good enough...

Sitting in my room... alone... my brain in overdrive... I was weighing up this massive decision. I didn't want to fail. I didn't want to be seen as a failure. But being a doctor... that's such a great achievement... that's what I should be. I mean, I'm good at science, and I want to help people... so that's the route I should go down...

BUT it wasn't what I expected.

BUT it wasn't what I wanted.

I was spending hours doing something that I wasn't passionate about, not wanting to disappoint others. If I'm a doctor, then everyone will be so proud of me. Maybe when I graduate, when I achieve that accolade, maybe then I would finally feel good enough?

The decision to leave medical school was a huge turning point – a painful learning curve, a taste of failure, but looking back... one I would not change.

Thinking back to my early teenage years, I was often found in my room singing at the top of my voice to all the classic tunes. One I often sang on repeat had a line that said: 'Why is everything so confusing? Maybe I'm just out of my mind...' Sometimes it feels like that, doesn't it!? So much confusion. So many decisions. Believing that if you make the wrong decision now, then you are doomed to fail.

Every decision does have a ripple effect on your life, but you are not doomed to fail. A stone dropped in a pond sends ripples in all directions, not just one. The choices we make do impact our lives; the skill is to adapt, learn new things, and then, we can change our path for the better.

It's hard at school sometimes, isn't it? Trying to make decisions when you're eleven, twelve, thirteen. Trying to think about what you want to be when you're older. What you want to do. There's so much pressure to know what you want to do. The 'older you' has seen that pressure and anxiety in her own students (yes... you actually become a teacher... not a doctor... but that's only part of your journey!)

You've seen teens being torn between what they actually enjoy and find interesting and expectations of what society sees as 'successful' and a well thought out career path. What if everyone chose what they enjoyed, what they were passionate about? What if everyone did that? Wouldn't the world be such a better place!

You got very competitive at school, even in primary school. You had a lovely group of friends who were all very high achieving, and you always wanted to be the best. Even at a young age, you tied part of your identity to the grades you achieved.

At secondary school, you wanted to be getting all those A*s at GCSE (9s these days). And you were surrounded by some very clever people, too. You wanted to be the best! I remember that childlike competitiveness of comparing who got the best marks in tests and who got to the extension questions in class.

The pressure intensified when you went to secondary school. It was a high-achieving private school, and you got in on a scholarship - an academic scholarship no less. So the pressure was there right from the start. There was a need to prove that you were worth that scholarship and that you would fulfil the expectation. Your parents have always encouraged you and championed you. They always wanted the best for you so that you could have loads of opportunities for later in life.

You had (and still have) high expectations of yourself – now that is both a good and a bad thing. It has given you a fierce determination and drive to not give up when things are tough, but it has also led to feelings of self-doubt. Feelings of not being good enough often creep in if you do not reach the high bar you set for yourself. You wanted to achieve everything you could and had the deep desire to make everyone proud.

You got the results you wanted, and when you got those grades, you felt that sense of pride. You got the praise. You got the recognition, and that helped you feel good. But what I've learnt since then is that if it's the praise that drives you, then any criticism can really hurt you and make you feel worthless.

If you find your identity in the opinions of others, or the grades on the paper, then you will never feel like you are enough. That is a lesson you will learn the hard way as you step out of med school, as you step out of teaching, as you start up your own business. If you constantly compare yourself to others or even compare yourself to your own extremely high standards, you will never be enough. You may be thinking, "Great, thanks for the encouragement," but the only way that you will feel enough is by separating your actual worth from your perception of what others think of you. FACT.

Growing up, you were quite shy and not very confident. People who know me now might think, "What?!" You've always been stubborn. Your stubbornness plays out in a couple of ways in later life... one being that you stand up for what you believe in (something that has been ingrained in you from your parents and grandparents). You always wanted to look out for those on the fringes of society; therefore, you were never part of the 'in-crowd.' You got bullied because of your 'rabbit' teeth. And that hurt you.

I wanted to feel accepted and validated but often looked to external sources rather than focusing on being enough just because I am me. Looking back, I can see that I sought validation through things such as boyfriends and my results. I was not secure in my identity, but being stubborn meant that it has taken me a long time to get to the point of realisation and to change what or whom I find my identity in!

You had never really experienced failure until you were 17. You took your driving test, and you failed. That was the first time that you didn't pass something. That was a shock. You didn't really know how to respond. You over-analysed every turn and mistake you made. Back then, you found your worth and identity in being a 'high achiever,' in being 'clever,' in being the person who 'doesn't fail.' That identity vanished at that moment. Failure was such a different feeling.

You are an interesting dichotomy of a people pleaser who doesn't want to disappoint anyone and also someone who is not afraid to stand up for what you believe in.

I remember standing in the middle of a circle with my friends all around, trying to persuade me to smoke weed. I stood my ground and never did. On the outside, I stayed strong, but internally, I took the taunts to heart.

Sometimes, you try to be strong for others and support them when actually, on the inside, you long for that support too. Sometimes, your strong-willed nature meant that you lost friends... and when you lost friends after sharing your opinions, that just confirmed the feeling of not being 'good enough.' You were left thinking that if you let your opinions out, then you would be rejected. As humans, we long to be accepted, and so rejection can feel like a knife through the soul. Our brains are programmed to keep us safe, so, therefore, we retreat into our shells.

When you hear comments that confirm your common internal thoughts, you often take them to heart. Even a comment said in jest can be over-analysed and remembered years on... 'Oh, you only just got an A in chemistry.' (Back then, an A was the highest grade you could get in your A Levels).

I was left thinking that even though I got the highest that I could, it wasn't enough. If you are in a state of worry or not feeling enough as you are reading this right now, you may have thoughts racing constantly through your brain. These common internal thoughts you have about yourself – often your 'go to' when you are feeling stressed - are called default thoughts. We all have them, and we must work intentionally to reframe them if our default thoughts are negative.

Try challenging them – why aren't you good enough? What's the evidence for that? And who defines what 'good enough' actually is anyway? There's this pressure we put on ourselves to be perfect. We compare our lives with other people and try to be a certain way just because society tells us that it is what you should do, but it doesn't make sense. Why can't we just focus on finding our joy?

Being happy takes priority over winning any competition or achieving an impressive result at school. You are a whole person, and exam results or things that you have achieved are only one piece of the puzzle – there's a whole lot more to discover.

So if you're not feeling good enough, if you're feeling beaten down by the pressure and the expectations of society or school, or parents, or friends, or yourself, then know that you have many skills and talents. Yes, maybe your skills and talents don't fit the social norms, but ask yourself this – do others get to define you? No, they don't.

For me, a defining moment was when I realised that my identity is not found in boyfriends, popularity, and results but that my identity is found in Jesus. Therefore, I should not care about comparing myself to others. Jesus loves me for who I am. I am unique, and he wants me to let my light shine. I am defined by my identity as a child of God.

Now, you may not believe in God, but either way, don't let your identity be defined by others. Work on what YOU are passionate about. Delve deep and think about what makes you happy. Start with something simple like writing down a list of what you like and don't like.

You can be that change that you want to see in the world. And that is why I'm writing this letter. I'm writing to encourage YOU to be the change that you want to see in your world. If we all do little things, take little steps in a positive direction, then we can be the ripple effect for positive change. If each one of us stands up and shares that we are not defined by our results and not defined by other people, then we can positively change the curvature of society.

We are often searching for a sense of belonging within society, and sometimes, we dim our lights to 'fit in.' I want you to know that what you have to offer the world is so valuable. I want you to shine your light brightly and let the world see you. It's hard if one of your default thoughts is that 'you are not good enough.' It is a thought I continue to tackle and reframe each day. You can't just flick a switch and wake up one day and never have those thoughts again, BUT with practice, bit by bit, you can challenge your default thought, change that thought, and choose to actually believe, 'I'm enough.' You don't need to be anyone else other than yourself... the world needs you!

Sitting in that room... alone... weighing up the big decision of whether to quit medical school and hearing that voice in your head saying, 'everyone will be disappointed in you if you quit.' You need to know that that voice isn't true.

The people who care about you are not disappointed in you; they love you and, therefore, want the best for you – you as a whole person. Unfortunately, sometimes that nagging voice in your head is very convincing! Not everything you think is true. Learn to challenge your thoughts, reframe them, and change the negative thought to a positive – because you definitely have the ability to do that! Positive thoughts will have a positive impact on your feelings, actions, and results.

A simple exercise I want you to try out is that when any negative thoughts come into your head, I want you to challenge them. I want you to think, "What is the basis of this thought? What are the facts? What is evidence against this thought?" Then, I want you to reframe the thought based on facts and evidence – choose to accept the new positive thought – that you are, in fact, good enough.

You, reading this letter, you may not feel like you are in the right place; you may not be feeling good enough. I want you to stop and pause; I want you to look back and see how far you have come, how every choice has rippled through in a positive way, and I want you to appreciate every little step. There are so many different opportunities and ways you can make a difference in life, but first, you need to accept yourself, find your identity, and then, you will be able to live as your full authentic self. And do me a favour ... tell that nagging voice in your head to shut up, and tell yourself that YOU ARE VALUABLE, and you ARE, in fact, MORE THAN enough!!

Love, Nicole

P.S. If you are into good singalong sessions like me, then go and pop on Defying Gravity! Don't accept those limits, and don't let others bring you down!

About Author

Nicole Bateman

Nicole is a mum of two, experienced teacher, creator of "A Box Full of Joy" and Co-Founder of "The Super Sensory Squad". She is passionate about supporting, encouraging, and empowering young people. Whilst teaching during the pandemic, she noticed an increase in anxiety in her students and widespread low self-esteem. Therefore, she started creating resources help young people to process their worries, communicate their feelings, and deal with overwhelm.

Her mentoring, stationery, letterbox gifts, and workshops enable anxious young people to become more resilient, confident, and calm. She wants to encourage teens to be the change they want to see in the world and equip parents with tools to support their teens to thrive like her book "My Child Has Exams...Now What?".

Nicole brought together authors from around the world to write Letters to my Teenage Self Volume Two to help teens feel seen in their struggles and give them hope for the future. She wants you, the reader, to know that what you have to offer the world is so valuable.

www.aboxfullofjoyuk.co.uk

www.thesupersensorysquad.com

www.instagram.com/a.box.full.of.joy.uk

www.instagram.com/thesupersensorysquad

Chapter Five

To the teen who self-harms

By Camila Piombini

To the teenager who self-harms,

Trigger warning: self-harm

The first time you did it, you didn't realise what had happened until you saw the marks and felt the sting on your skin.

On the surface you look like quite an ordinary fifteen-year-old. You love listening and dancing to the latest music, hanging out with your friends and talking about your crushes. But you have already been through a lot at this age, and the road is about to get even more bumpy.

You moved from Brazil to England without speaking one word of English at eleven years old. The first few years were tough. You attended a school with very little diversity where you were seen by many as an anomaly, something that didn't belong. Sometimes their words echoed in your head like they were your own inner voice. The teachers couldn't pronounce your name, you couldn't understand or express yourself, and the other students saw you as an easy target. This is hard when you're a teen. It sparked up a lot of bullying for a couple of years. Name-calling, physical aggression and even spitting. You just wanted to understand why it was happening. It must be you. You must be missing something that others had. Make-up? Straight hair? Shorter skirts? An English accent? Well, you worked very hard on a lot of those things. Anything to help you fit in and disappear into the background. Things changed after a couple of years when you moved to a different school with your new English accent and your new self-identity.

You did OK at fitting in there. You had friends, not many, but some. You found your passion for performing on stage. Taking on a character's personality and having permission to be silly, or angry, or in love, and it was all OK because you were acting it out in someone else's words. This boosted your confidence enough to carry on for a few years.

Now you're fifteen. There is a fierce battle inside of you. With every perceived failure, come the thoughts about what you're lacking. How can the others do it so well? How do they find it so easy? Why is it OK for them but not OK for me? What am I missing?

The voices inside you just keep on arguing. You're good, but not good enough. People tolerate you, but they don't understand you. Your family loves you, but they must not care that much about you. The critical voice gets louder and louder. YOU ARE NOT ENOUGH. It screams and blocks out anything else going on in your head.

You're crying because this voice won't shut up. You feel the emotions taking over your body, so you cry harder. You step into the shower in an attempt to distract yourself, but the pain inside feels like it has a mind of its own. It wants to get out. Your hands tense up and your nails become weapons. You scratch your bare skin, and you don't know why. It feels good to experience pain on the outside, distracting from the hurting inside. It feels out of control, all the rage and hurt and sadness gather at your fingertips and glide through your skin like blades.

You snap out of it for a moment and notice what happened. It scares you. What just happened? As you dry yourself you look at the marks. Oh, you hadn't thought about the marks. All the way down your arms, and body. Some on your neck. It will be hard to hide this.

People ask what happened but you don't want to talk about it. You make up a quick lie about playing with your puppy. Some people believe you, others don't. It just feels like nobody really understands. You experience both pity and anger from the people who know. You just want to tell them that you don't understand it either, but the shame and fear keeps you silent.

I'm now you twenty years later. I can tell you that what happened was a form of self-harming. Some people cut themselves with blades. Some people burn themselves. Some people bite and hit themselves, or punch and kick things that are so hard it will hurt them. Deliberately causing pain to yourself is self-harming. We hurt ourselves in many ways in the past, but just know that we are now free from it. It took a while, but I am free.

Self-harming can happen when internal emotions get extremely intense. They gather momentum and it can feel unbearably overwhelming. I would then hurt myself in an attempt to externalise that feeling and to be in control of that pain. It could distract me enough to allow me to get on with my day.

The trouble is that once my body learnt this as a coping strategy to extreme emotional pain, it went back to it much more quickly the next time. And the time after that. And the time after that. Until it felt like I couldn't help it, because it seemed like it was out of my control.

It's so hard to talk about it, isn't it? I've heard people saying that those who self-harm are just trying to get attention. I felt so much shame for what I did, and that shame held my voice hostage. I was scared that if people found out what was really happening, they'd judge me; or they'd say I was doing it for attention; or they might have thought I was suicidal, which I wasn't. That's not what any of it was ever about. They might have told me to just stop doing it, as if I had a choice.

One thing I can tell you now is that there is hope. The urges to self-harm are linked to mental illness which can be treated and managed. Shame gains strength in hiding and silence, but it loses its power once you reach out to someone who responds with care and empathy. With the help of therapy, the urges subsided, and I felt strong enough to make better choices when they arose. There is no magic cure, it does take time and willpower to work, but the result of feeling in control of my emotions is absolutely worth it.

As a teen I shared my painful experiences in counselling sessions, which really helped to calm my urges and control the emotional pain at the time. But the truth is that I held back and never truly exposed everything. I still feared being judged by others because I judged myself too. Because of this I carried this mental illness all the way to my adult years, allowing the shame to grow bigger, and cover vast spaces inside me.

I carried this secret for so long that it just became part of me. It got easier to hide the marks and I learnt to only ever do it when I was alone, usually in the middle of the night. When the morning came I pushed it out of my mind. As long as I didn't talk about it, it was like it never existed. The trouble was that the urges got stronger and more frequent, and it felt like I was losing my mind. I had a toddler and a new baby to care for by then and, even though this was only ever directed at myself, I knew this behaviour was getting too scary and out of control. That's when I broke the silence. I reached out to my most trusted person, the one who would never judge or accuse me. I opened up to my sister just enough to admit that I needed help. That was the first difficult and scary step towards healing.

Fast-forward a few months, and my therapist asked me boldly "why do you hate yourself?". I was so shocked at that. Me? Hate myself? You clearly don't know me, lady. I am the most positive and optimistic person you'll find. I love and help everyone, how can I not love me? I just need to find a better way of dealing with my emotions, that's all!

But that question played on my mind for many weeks to come, and deep down I found the buried emotions from when I didn't feel like I was enough. Not good enough, not pretty enough, not clever enough. My eyes opened and that's when the magic happened. Those wounds needed to be exposed before they could be treated and healed. I was a thirty-two-year-old woman, holding on to an 11-year-old girl's feelings. I needed to let her know that I saw her. She'd believed the lies in her head, but thoughts are not facts. I had to remind her of everything she had done to prove just how strong she really was. That strength helped to quiet down the critical voices in my head and fill the spaces with hope, faith, determination, gratitude and little specks of joy. I built so much love and respect for myself that the little things just didn't bother me anymore. I let go of my need to please other people and put them before my own basic needs. I understood that before I could help someone else, I first needed to work on myself - like putting on my oxygen mask first before I can help anyone else in an emergency.

I know that much of the advice out there for young people who struggle with self-harm is focused on distraction, like listening to music or going for a walk; or redirection such as drawing on your skin with a red marker, or flicking an elastic band on your wrist. All this advice is valid and useful, but it is also superficial and temporary. True healing comes from digging down into the root of the problem and dealing with it at the source. When a plant experiences root rot, it can make healthy leaves turn a different colour or their sturdy stems go dry and brittle. Similarly, roots of guilt, shame, grief, loneliness and other emotional issues can present themselves in behaviour changes such as self-harming, anger outbursts and isolation. The process of digging, revealing and pruning the bad roots is not easy nor pleasant, but once it sees daylight it loses its controlling power and gives room for transformation. Taking the first step and opening up can be difficult, but it's an important part of getting help and feeling better. Once pruned, the plant can then be placed into new soil. This may come in the form of new habits, new environments or just the opportunity for a clean slate – to allow it to heal, grow and thrive. It's important to find someone you trust and feel comfortable talking to; whether it's an adult, friend, relative, teacher, or professional. There are people who can help and support you.

Personally, this pruning process meant understanding that the truths about myself that I'd held on to for so long, were flawed. From there I started to practise more introspection to find out who I really was and who I wanted to be. It also meant being kind to myself, which may sound like an inspirational quote you read on social media, but this new habit saved me. I changed the way I spoke to myself inside my head and gave myself room to make mistakes. This new insight allowed me to become stronger than I've ever been. Now I am able to use this new knowledge to help other teenagers, just like you, to accept who they truly are and take care of their own roots, so that they too can display healthy and positive behaviours for many years to come. I have become the adult you needed when it all started in your teenage years. What a true transformation. Remember you don't have to go through difficult times alone, and seeking help is a sign of strength.

All my love, Camila

About Author

Camila Piombini

Camila was born in Brazil and has been living in the south coast of England for over 23 years. With more than a decade of experience teaching in secondary schools, Camila has a passion for working closely with young people. Her years of volunteering as a youth leader have inspired her to pursue further qualifications, including becoming a Youth Mental Health First Aider, an NLP practitioner focused on children and young people, and training for a crisis line with Young Minds charity.

Camila's unique blend of mental health knowledge and her ability to connect and communicate with young people has led her to become an Emotional Wellbeing Coach for teenagers. Specialising in raising self-esteem, she helps young people overcome mental health challenges and find confidence in themselves.

When she's not working, Camila loves to move her body in Pilates classes or enjoy dance parties with her two young children.

https://www.facebook.com/prismawellbeing

https://www.instagram.com/prismawellbeing

linkedin.com/in/camila-piombini-311142b4

Chapter Six

To the teen whose world got turned upside down

By Louise Plunkett

To the teen whose world got turned upside down,

'You were right, there is something wrong with your daughter's eyes. She's going blind, but there's nothing we can do. Have a lovely Christmas and we'll see you in the clinic in January."

Two sentences that changed my world forever - I was fifteen.

I had been ping ponging between my optician and the paediatric eye consultant at my local hospital for a number of years. I was struggling to read the board at school and had missed an entire section of a maths test as I didn't see it on the overhead projector screen. Teachers were constantly telling me I needed glasses as I always held textbooks so close to my face to be able to read them.

My optician described examining the retinas of my eyes as "looking at the eyes of a much older person". He was puzzled. There was no need for a prescription to correct my vision, yet I couldn't read as far down on the eye chart as expected. I couldn't do the Ishihara colour blindness mosaic tests, but was able to successfully complete the more complex colour testing at hospital.

The paediatric eye consultant who I saw every three to six months, described me as "an enigma", a mystery, but was nonplussed as to what was wrong. It felt almost as though I was making the issues up. I was an only child, and indirectly, he told my parents that they had all their eggs in one basket and were perhaps being neurotic about my vision. He humoured us as a family but wasn't prepared to delve deeper to discover why I now had to sit at the front row of desks at school to peer at the board, or why my previously accurate hand-eye coordination was rapidly getting worse.

The frequent trips to the hospital for appointments during school time were a source of humour amongst my peers. -I didn't really have any close friends, but I was friendly with lots of people. I was sporty, I played on the school netball team and a team outside of school. -I had given up playing competitive badminton for my county, as my performance had dropped significantly. I missed more shots than I actually hit and was frustrated and embarrassed that I was no longer able to play, but didn't know why. I felt disappointment from all angles that I couldn't play like I used to. When summer rolled around and it was rounders season, I was no longer able to hit the ball at all.

My visual world was changing and nothing made any sense. Being fobbed off by the hospital only made me feel like I was a freak. Mental health wasn't a topic discussed much back in the 1990's and I was beginning to wonder if I was imagining it all.

So, in December of 1994, I finally underwent electro diagnostic testing, after my parents in frustration pushed the consultant for other testing to be done, to discover why I was having so many issues. "Well there are, but they aren't very pleasant. Do you really want to put your daughter through that?" was his response.

The tests involved having very fine electric wires placed in my eye socket under my lower lids, electrodes stuck to my head, and being sat in a makeshift testing booth. It was a windowless records room in the hospital. A blackout sheet was placed over the door once I was hooked up to the equipment. I sat in total darkness for twenty minutes. It was hot and stuffy and I could smell the shelves of crammed papers all around me.

I then endured lots of bright lights flashing in my eyes for varying periods of time. Some I had to follow with my eyes without moving my head, others I had to force my eyes to stay open, as multiple bright flashes continually popped an inch from my face. Imagine how it feels when you unexpectedly get a camera flash - it was like that but more concentrated, repeated for what seemed like endless minutes at a time. When the ordeal was over, I returned to school to complete my day. I was in year 10 and was immersed in studying for GCSEs. I was a diligent pupil, always completing homework on time, and when I had appointments, I would always ask for the work I'd missed so I could catch-up.

When my Mum received the call that I did in fact have a rare genetic eye disease that was incurable and untreatable, I felt relief.

Relief that I wasn't making this up.

Relief that finally I had an answer.

Relief that I wasn't a freak. Although this changed as I became the object of fascination at school.

The one thing that hit me hardest when I saw a different consultant the following year, the only one who was qualified to interpret the electro diagnostic testing and had only recently started working at my local hospital, was the fact that my eyesight was already too poor for me to ever drive a car.

I had a part time weekend job, working as a kitchen assistant at a local hotel, and I was saving my wages towards driving lessons and buying my first car, a classic Mini. Following diagnosis it was decided that working in a busy, hot and hazard filled kitchen wasn't the best place for me, so I had to leave.

An empathetic bedside manner wasn't something he had clearly learned or developed during his training. "You can't drive a car; you've lost too much vision already. You can't fly a plane or drive a train, but other than that, go and get on with your life. I'm registering you as blind, you'll be allocated a social worker, but I don't need to see you again." And that was that.

Smartphones didn't exist back then; the internet was in its infancy with limited access. As a family unit of 3, we literally had nothing, until we heard from the social worker. And that in itself created a sense of shame, fear and unease. Social workers were for those families with domestic issues, not one like ours. It felt like a huge stigma to be assigned my own social worker.

My high school was brilliant, they were so supportive and accommodating. They did everything they could to help me with my learning, at such a crucial time. My timetable was reviewed, as were my GCSE options that I was four months into. Decisions were made at meetings for my focus to be on core subjects, and the option of art that I loved and had chosen was dropped, due to the sheer number of hours it took me each week to complete homework. Design Technology was another that I dropped, as safety was the priority, and it was deemed I would've been better putting my time, energy and efforts into the other subjects. This meant I had the opportunity for extra study time at school. A classroom was available for me to go to where I could switch the lights off, rest if eye strain was an issue, or continue with work in order to keep up to speed with the rest of my classes. It had been taking me longer and longer to complete work in those months because I had such high standards for what I produced.

As I've mentioned, I played a number of sports competitively - netball, rounders, and I had already given up badminton. Now we knew why. But the biggest blow was yet to come.

I had played on the school netball team, and in the same team outside of school for over 3 years, and we were very successful. I was a goalkeeper and had never been a reserve player. But one day when I checked the team list for an upcoming match, my name wasn't there. Not even on the reserve list. There had been no conversation with me about this. It was as if my diagnosis meant that I was no longer good enough to be part of the team. I was devastated, but I didn't tell anyone how hurt, rejected and worthless I felt. I then found out that the team I played with outside of school had also dropped me. Again, no discussion, I found out by overhearing a conversation between a couple of the other girls on the team that they were off to a tournament.

More rejection, pain, hurt, humiliation.

It was a bitter pill to swallow.

The only upside was that both teams were no longer as successful moving forwards after I had been dropped.

Life at school carried on. I had been assigned by my social worker, a chap whose title was 'peripatetic teacher for the blind'. He promised so much support and equipment, but, just like the other professionals, both medical and in social care, was yet another big let down. When it came to my first set of mock GCSEs, he assured me that he would be there for my first one to act as my reader, and scribe should I need it.

I sat waiting nervously at my tiny exam desk. I waited. The exam started. I waited some more. -Eventually I decided to just get on with it and vowed that I would no longer rely on anyone else. If I needed something to be done, I'd figure out a way of doing it myself. He eventually showed up as I was going into my allocated extra time for the exam.

One thing he did do though, was to come into my form group, and explain what vision loss was like. He brought a selection of simulation specs with him, which gives the wearer an indication of what various eye conditions are like. I can vividly remember a girl in the class saying "oh it's not too bad, you can just look out from the bottom of these or the sides". Perhaps simulation goggles would be more accurate.

In some classes I sat at the front, sometimes at the teachers desk when we were copying from the board. For a girl who was shy, not particularly outgoing and who would never put her hand up voluntarily to answer questions, this was really hard for me. In fact I'd go as far as saying I hated it. I hated having everyone's eyes on me, I could feel them burning into the back of my head.

Any time I got out my pocket magnifying glass to enable me to read worksheets or textbooks more easily, it would end up being passed around the room so everyone could 'have a go'. I would smile and allow it to happen, but inside I was just cringing. I just wanted to disappear, to be invisible and to just get on with my work. The same would happen if I used my monocular, a small telescope for reading the board. Again, this would be passed around. I would smile and laugh with them, patiently waiting for it to come back to me.

When worksheets started arriving on A3 paper compared to everyone else's A4, and on pink paper as it had less glare than white for me, it was yet another opportunity for me to become the centre of attention. The questions, the jokes, the overwhelming feeling of being different, not fitting in, being an outsider, and very much feeling like an exhibit at the zoo.

I started symbol cane training. I received the cane from my local sight loss charity as a result of being registered partially sighted, now known as sight impaired. A few months later because of my vision deteriorating, I was registered as blind, now known as severely sight impaired. My mobility instructor initially started training me around my school. However, this prompted yet more blunt questions as students from all year groups would see me out of classroom windows, and would come up to me at break and lunchtimes, or in the corridors and ask "are you blind then or what? You don't look it". I learnt very quickly to develop an armour for these questions, and would politely answer, but inside I was willing them to go away and leave me alone.

Whilst I didn't have any close friends, I was friendly with lots of people, and during those last two years at high school, was asked if I was going to the city at the weekend or going skating at the local rink. I so wanted to go, but I had more barriers to being able to socialise than my peers.

Looking back now, and as a parent myself, I can understand my own parents' reluctance and fear in letting me go out.

There were no mobile phones, no ability to track my whereabouts on an app, and as an only child, they felt deeply responsible for having passed on a genetic disease with a probability of one in four of inheriting it. Luck wasn't with me.

I used to love riding my bike, we had a cycle path near where we lived which I loved riding along. One day I came home from school and went out to the garage to get my bike out, but it wasn't there. My parents told me that they had sold it, because I was no longer safe out riding it. Just like I wasn't safe to go out and meet up with friends at the weekend. The justification was that it wasn't fair on my friends to be responsible for my safety when crossing roads, and that they wouldn't be thinking about looking out for me.

So my world became very small. I went to school and then came home. I didn't see anyone outside of school. I felt as though I was wrapped in cotton wool, had been put into a cage like a bird and the door locked.

When I did go out, it was always with either or both of my parents. We joined a couple of national charities associated with sight loss and attended the local support groups. But I was the youngest there. By decades. And that in itself was alienating. Somewhere else where I didn't fit in, where I felt painfully aware that I wasn't like all the other teens out there. I felt like a freak, a weirdo, an alien. I had nobody to talk to at all, because I couldn't voice my frustrations, loneliness and feelings to my parents out of respect for them. They were just doing what felt right, to protect me and keep me safe. I was sent a list of people who I could ring to chat to about my sight loss, but again, there was at least a 45 year plus age gap, so I felt there was nothing in common, as these people had all lost their sight in later life. None of them were facing it as a teen.

So I buried myself in my school work, my exam revision and then the exams themselves. I didn't go onto sixth form, having experienced negative attitudes from staff towards me. Asking if I came with my own photocopying budget, and even having one teacher physically backing away from me as though my sight loss was contagious. Instead I attended my local FE college to study A levels, where there was a fantastic support team for students with disabilities.

Anxiety and panic attacks, however, became a staple in my life at this time. I felt huge pressure to blend in, to be "normal", as I was desperate to make solid friendships. I was on my own at college as my peers had stayed at sixth form, so I was in effect starting afresh. I received mobility training again to teach me the safest route to walk up to college from the bus stop. I chose not to use my symbol cane at college as I didn't want to be a target for yet more snide comments, or the butt of jokes. The workload for me was huge, as it took me hours to complete my studies each week. One of my tutors was shocked at how long it took me. But I ploughed on, determined not to give up.

And that has been my ethos throughout life, don't give up. Even when life and situations are so incredibly tough and challenging, I kept going. I battled with anxiety and depression throughout my late teens, had group support sessions, medication and doctor's appointments. Again, mental health support was a stigma in the late 1990's, so I felt mortified and ashamed that I needed to access these services. And again, there was no one going through sight loss or near my own age at those sessions, nobody who I could relate to at all. It was a lonely world I was living in.

I developed a chronic illness when I was nineteen, ME/CFS, a result of pushing my body too far physically with training and competing at a high level at swimming. I had been talent spotted at a disabled swimming group, was encouraged to join a club, receive coaching and compete. I had finally found a sport that I could follow that didn't require a team, and I was good at it. I began to get a name for myself within the disability swimming circuit, as I regularly competed at competitions and equalled or bettered the performance of those already in the GB visually impaired squad. My goal was to represent my country at the Sydney 2000 Paralympics, and my competition times were getting closer and closer to the qualifying times needed for the trials.

I felt the pressure. Suddenly again I was being watched, was the centre of attention, and it skyrocketed my anxiety to a whole new level, which impacted on my ability to eat, sleep and function. Yet again, my life didn't feel like it was in my control, that other adults were making all the decisions and I was on autopilot. I had finished my A levels at this point and took a gap year to concentrate on my swimming more, as it required a lot of time both in the pool and in the gym, travel and planning. I felt like a hamster stuck on a wheel with no opportunity to get off, and nobody to talk with who would be impartial and I could safely offload onto, without causing offence or upset.

I appeared in my local newspaper several times, with full page articles and photos, and the pressure I felt ramped up more notches. I constantly felt nauseous, stressed, on edge, trapped. But I couldn't tell anyone. "Mind over matter" was a phrase I heard a lot, but what did that even mean? I had no toolkit of coping strategies, the only release I felt was when I got so anxious and stressed that I vomited. The panic attacks were happening more and more frequently, I felt consumed by them, totally out of control.

And then one day the hamster wheel broke. I woke up two days after a competition and wasn't able to get out of bed. I was beyond exhausted, had flu like symptoms, would sleep for seventeen hours around the clock but wake still feeling exhausted. Glandular fever was initially suspected, but blood tests proved otherwise. In fact, nothing showed up in any of the blood work I had done over the following months. Eventually ME/CFS was diagnosed. And that was the end of my swimming dream.

The intense pressure I had been living under, the physical and mental strain I had put my body through, pushing through cold after cold, had all come to a head. 'No more' was my body's message. I cried with relief that I was off the hamster wheel that I had once thought I wanted to be on.

Ahead of me lay a very long road, not to recovery, but to management and learning to live with the daily constant physical, neurological, mental and emotional symptoms.

But I've made it. Now in my forties, my sight has deteriorated further still, but I have found ways to work with it. I manage my ME/CFS symptoms, alongside running a home, having 2 children, and I've been married for over twenty years. I didn't fully embrace my sight loss until the last few years though. As a new mum I was terrified that my baby would be taken away from me if I was seen to not be coping. So I tried so hard to be like all the other mums I met at baby and toddler groups, and then in the school playground. Yes it was challenging when there were days out planned with school friends in the holidays because I couldn't drive. Logistics had to be worked out. I hated having to ask for lifts, as I felt it made me less of a mum somehow.

I have a strong core friendship group of mums who accepted me for who I was, didn't patronise me, were supportive and helpful. There are always people like that out there, it can just take a while to find them.

And now I have a phenomenal circle of women around me, all business owners, because little old me, the girl who had no idea what she wanted to do with her life, now has her own business. Turning my experiences into a positive and educating businesses on how to create accessible and inclusive digital content. I've stepped into my power and turned my disability into an awesome ability to teach others and make the world a more accessible place for the visually impaired community globally.

Instead of hiding my sight loss, I'm very much a proud advocate for sharing my experiences, and the adventures I go on with my long white cane who I've called Michael Cane. And yes I use the catchphrase "don't mess with me!" I embrace my disability and instead of viewing it as a negative, I've flipped it into a positive to help and inspire others.

As for my anxiety and panic attacks, they have dwindled. I now have a toolkit of coping strategies I've built up over the years. I've taken back control of how I respond to stressful situations, to the point where the attacks are a rarity. It's not easy but it can be achieved.

Never stop believing in yourself and your abilities.

Keep moving forward, no matter how slow the progress.

The end destination is the same as those in the fast lane, but take the scenic route, it's much more interesting and rewarding.

About Author

Louise Plunkett

Louise Plunkett is a wife and mum of two boys. She lives with a genetic, progressive and incurable eye disease. This has caused her to lose the majority of her central vision. Louise is passionate about raising awareness and sharing the importance of improved digital accessibility and inclusion with businesses. She has been instrumental in making positive changes from small independents through to global organisations. She uses the frustrations she experiences on a daily basis to educate others on the simple changes they can make, in order to be more inclusive.

Louise always shares and teaches from the heart, giving an insight into her life and challenges that she encounters. She also uses this experience in her volunteer role as a telephone befriender with the Macular society, a UK based charity supporting those living with sight loss. At a local level, she volunteers with another charity, working with children, young people and their families to facilitate, access and enjoy activities, as well as being a positive role model for living with sight loss.

https://www.facebook.com/groups/460274282695583/

http://www.Instagram.com/impact.with.lou

https://www.linkedin.com/in/louise-plunkett-659589183

Chapter Seven

To the teen who doesn't have it all together

By Janice Watson

To the teen who doesn't have it altogether,

I want to share a story with you. It's about a girl just like you. She feels like she's falling apart. She feels responsible for everyone else's feelings. The bullies have discovered that she is the odd one out. She feels like nobody could possibly understand her or what she's been through. She feels like she's lived an extraordinary life (in a bad way) already. She feels like everyone else has it all figured out - what they're doing and where they're headed in life.

She is so desperate to fit in. So desperate to be loved. So desperate to have someone by her side, to save and support her. So desperate for security and stability.

The girl in the story is me.

I grew up in a broken family. Mum left dad after a big argument, taking my half-brother and I with her. The experience left me feeling responsible. Responsible for their happiness over my own. Feeling like I had to keep the peace for everyone's safety. Feeling like I had to do what I should do, even if I wasn't sure what that was.

I spent my young life bouncing between mum's house, mum's boyfriend's house and dad's house. Mum moved around a lot, so in the early days I had to sleep in mum's bed as there was no space for me. Mum's boyfriend's house was cold, damp and full of cigarette smoke. Dad's house was really my step-mum's house - I had a room that doubled as my dad's storeroom, and I'd often have to clear the bed so that I wasn't sleeping on panes of glass or sawdust.

It really felt like I had no space among the chaos.

Mum and dad were so busy floundering in their own lives that I felt that they didn't really notice me.

School was a boring routine and I felt unchallenged by the curriculum. The academic work was so much easier to understand and cope with than the social aspect of life. I was the odd one out that liked to learn and the awkward one at the party, where I couldn't hear what was being said and was too embarrassed to dance with everyone watching.

This left me vulnerable to the bullies that saw the sad, unconfident, withdrawn girl I was as a weakness to be mocked. I was desperate to believe in something or someone that could save me. Someone that could take care of me, make me feel safe, loved and supported.

When I met my first proper boyfriend at age fourteen, it seemed like I finally had that someone. He was a little older, confident, fun and carefree. I wanted to be like that! So, I held on to him. I took on his beliefs, let him have all the power in the relationship. He was decent and kind, so it was really good for a while.

While my peers were partying and having friendship dramas, having an older boyfriend gave me an excuse to avoid the parties that I wasn't even invited to. It was exciting hanging out with him, talking about nothing and everything, watching TV, listening to music. Being with him was fun and easy. When I felt safe, I was more confident.

He left school and began a computing apprenticeship which enabled him to have money of his own. I still had no idea what I wanted to do with my life so I latched onto some vague idea of being an engineer that I thought would impress everyone. Since my dad had an engineering background, I thought it was something I could do.

A teacher once told me that going to university offered the potential to find other people just like me, so when we visited a university not so far from home that offered a course I was interested in, I applied and received a provisional offer. It meant that I could stay living at dad's and not having to break up with my boyfriend. The plan was set.

I had sailed through the subjects needed at GCSE level, so I didn't expect it to be difficult at A level.

But I was woefully unprepared for the work required. As it all got too much, I started skipping classes. There was one person that could see that I was struggling, and they tried to encourage me to attend. But in my panic, I was adamant that it would be better to revise what I'd already been taught. I couldn't see the point of trying to take more in when I couldn't regurgitate enough for the exams as it was.

My worst fears came true when I sat in my exams and realised I'd never seen these types of questions before. Waiting for the inevitable dire results was torture. What was I going to do if I failed? It had been hard enough coming up with this plan.

The results were proof to me that I was a failure. I'd failed my exams, so I wasn't worthy of respect. I couldn't go to the university that I had chosen and make the friends that I'd been promised.

I let everyone down and was even less understood than before! Dad just laughed when I showed him the results - maybe a nervous thing, but I felt even more of a failure. Mum said that she only wanted me to do my best, but I felt that she thought I'd failed her too.

It felt like the end of the world. What was I going to do? I'd wasted two years of my life studying with nothing to show for it. What university would want me now? What employer would consider someone that had nothing to show for the last two years.

But you know what? It wasn't the end of the world. Failing those exams simply meant that a change of direction was needed. Those subjects were not right for me at that time of my life. The reasons for choosing that path were not right, and I had learnt so much about myself.

Failure meant becoming relatable to others that didn't do as well as they were expecting. Failure meant that school failed me.

It didn't mean that I couldn't go to university. It didn't mean that no employer would want me. It did mean that I had to find a new plan.

So I've learned that it's OK to choose something new. Despite what they've been telling you or what you've thought, the choices you make now are not set in stone. You can change your mind; you can change your path.

Choosing difficult subjects doesn't justify your worth. You are worthy whatever you choose. You don't need to justify yourself.

I've also learned and want to tell you that you are loved and loveable, even if you feel that you're not. Even if you feel the shame of failure.

I've learned that I am stronger than I think, and that I can be the best friend that will always be there - for myself. You can be that one person that always understands and knows everything about you and STILL loves you. Yeah, I know it sounds a little 'out there'. Is it any more out there than believing that you're a failure, or believing in a higher power? One that controls everything. One that, if exists, has allowed so much pain and suffering in the world. But YOU do exist. You are alive. You are an amazing person. Look how far you've come already.

I've learned that I've always kept pushing to find 'success'. I have learned that the people I was trying to impress were not even worthy - everyone has their demons. I have learned that taking a break from trying so hard brings better results. If you do 'you', everything falls into place.

I have learned that I can only be responsible for myself. I can only be responsible for how I react to situations. I can't control anyone else or how they feel, no matter how hard I try. This is a difficult one for me and I must remind myself over and over!

Reflecting on what went wrong highlights the need to accept myself as I am. To listen to myself, and what I want, rather than trying to please everyone else.

I have learned that not everyone has, and I STILL don't have it figured out. And it's OK.

So, I want you to know that you are more capable than you think. You are strong and worthy. Keep pushing forward and never give up on yourself.

Sincerely, Me x

About Author

Janice Watson

Jan Watson is a multi-passionate female entrepreneur, with a husband, twin teenagers and two cats. Jan is on a mission to help children enjoy learning the future-proof skill of computing. She does this by facilitating fun activities where children get to choose how to explore their interests without overwhelm or pressure. Jan wants children to know that their opinion is important. She stands against prescriptive teaching and memorisation of facts and encourages creativity and innovation. Inspiring one learner at a time.

https://www.facebook.com/scooshlive

www.Scoosh.live

Chapter Eight

To the teen who wants to challenge the status quo

By Param Kaur-Kingston

To the teen who wants to challenge the status quo

You are an Indian Sikh and grew up in a very traditional but strict loving home with your parents. They arrived in the UK when they were thirteen and had an arranged marriage to each other when they were about eighteen. You grew up with four older brothers and one older sister in a small, predominantly white community. The Indian community you grew up in tends to see the woman's position in the home as typically traditional and passive, and often a role that is considered less important than men. Introduced marriages and following family traditions was the 'done thing'.

As a twelve-year-old, you were bright, intelligent, passionate, and deserved more in life than getting married to a suitor. You are proud of your faith but do not need to get married to prove that. All your older siblings went along with the plan that was set for them. You didn't know what to do.

You loved living in a big house with all your older siblings, nephews, and nieces but being the youngest was often frustrating. Your parents worked extremely hard to provide for you all. You all had responsibilities to work in the family business, but it was hard to have so many duties at that age, and the expectation of an arranged marriage once you left school was heavy.

You are not going to let history repeat itself. You want to avoid this happening to you. You are pleased that your parents' ‘arranged marriage worked out and your brothers', but you will struggle with marrying someone you do not know or respect. You have more to give the world than to be someone's wife! But are you just fighting a losing battle? You didn't want to leave school at sixteen and be matched to a suitor. You refused to be measured in life by doing everything expected of you.

Women already have less say in the community. You are expected to be passive, not to openly question the status quo, and told not to do anything that might disgrace the community.

You knew you could get through to your parents that you want your education to come first, and for girls to have the same opportunities as the boys in the family. Just because all your siblings agreed to an introduced or arranged marriage doesn't mean you have to. You wanted to try a new path on your own but without disappointing others.

There was so much judgement in our small Indian community, and growing up in a small town, everyone knows everything. There was not much integration by the wider Sikh community but my family was known and are very well liked because they had a local business and assimilated well with the wider community.

-

I hated the judgements, gossip, and the stares you got when you were out in public with your mum. You always wore conservative clothing like jeans and t-shirts but the gazing eyes of the community made you feel uncomfortable. You felt like you had two heads. You could not grasp speaking Punjabi very fluently but understood every word of it. People made fun of you with the broken Punjabi, so you stopped trying to practise it because you feared being laughed at.

You were about thirteen when your siblings started to get introduced marriages, one every year for about three years. You started to confuse the culture and tradition here with religion and you felt so conflicted.

You witnessed aunts in the communities beaming when their young daughters had suitors. It was shameful how parents were being measured as 'successful parents' by how many children they had married off.

You always battled with putting only half effort into homework, as you know the expectation was to agree to an arranged marriage at some point, so did it matter? You felt the strain of the family's reputation to do the right thing, not disappoint anyone, or disgrace the family. You knew you needed to speak up.

You were jealous of your brother who was always going out with his friends, his clothing didn't get questioned, he didn't have chores, and he came home whenever he wanted to, rather than learning to make chapatis. It made you cross. There was one rule for the boys and another rule for the girls. It felt so unequal. You used to wish you were a boy as it would have been easier. When boys were born, the community would throw a party, yet girls were not celebrated in the same way.

You visited your sister when you were thirteen and she was nineteen. She had agreed to an arranged marriage to someone she met once, and the second time was on her wedding day. There were more than one family living in one house, and she had a lot of expectations of her to be a submissive daughter-in-law and wife. She was trying her best to please the in-laws and her husband, but you were not confident she was happy, as her smile had faded. She said she was fine, but you could see in her eyes she was sad and missed her home. She was losing weight and you could see she had the lost the fight in her that she had before she got married and it was far from what she expected living in a home full of people who were treating her poorly had taken its toll.

You realised you did not want to end up having this life. It would be scary leaving everything familiar behind and not being able to study and have a career. You know this is the custom you come from, but the boys in your family got the chance to pursue careers, jobs, or education and make something of themselves without too much judgement. You wanted that too.

Your sister is seven years older than you and was by your side until she got married and moved to London. She protected you in many ways but she was no longer living with you and didn't visit often.

She didn't have the ability to say no to the wedding. What made you think you could stop this for your life? She never took any crap when she worked in the family business, often dealing with challenging customers; and you never saw her allow anyone to talk down to her. Where had that voice gone now, to speak up? Her environment wounded her self-esteem. You had to try and be her voice and support her.

This was when you became determined, despite not feeling smart enough to get any GCSEs, or bright enough to get A levels, or to go to university and see the world (because girls do not do this from your community). This spurred you on to show your community there is a bright and wonderful brain contained in your head.

When it came to expressing an interest in further education it was also to delay the inevitable, a. A family member told your parents "Get her married as soon as possible. She will only disappoint you and get out of hand"". This cut like a sword. You knew your parentshad to believe in you and accept you were capable of more. You would overhear conversations about potential suitors and my family were asked if we would consider meeting families[1] so something could be set in stone for the future. You knew your mum was sent pictures for your mum to consider. It made you sick to the stomach at the thought of it! You were petrified that you would be unhappily living miles away from anything familiar. You masked this by threatening to pick any of the suitors marry and then divorce him. You knew this was seen as shameful by the family and was told it could affect the suitors your nieces and nephews would get. It was a lot of pressure.

When you would try to speak up, you would get told to 'shh' and to be more submissive and told it's the done thing to do it this way. It made you so cross. On top of that members of the community would say you were not tall enough, too dark-skinned, or not pretty enough for their sons. But they were no match for you!

You desperately longed for someone in the same boat to be challenging the status quo.

Secondary school was not very easy, you didn't feel very well-liked or popular in school. You were conscious that it was the colour of your skin. No one believed you when you told the class that two masked robbers with a knife robbed your family store. Your dad fought one of them off whilst the other held his hand over your mouth as I ran for the store phone to call the police. It was an extremely frightening experience that taught you just how courageous you are.

You leaned heavily on your relationship with your sister, and one of your brothers, who you knew could help you navigate the path to further education. You knew you needed to pass all of your GCSEs but you really struggled to write and spell, and never had the confidence to ask for more help in class. You also found maths to be a real struggle and you felt so different. It hurt even deepwhen you were called 'thick'.

You got an E in GCSE maths and were devastated. You were determined not to let it define you. You got to sixth form and promised to resit the maths exam. You panicked that you wouldn't be able to get further education without maths. You were grateful mum spent money on a private tutor to help you. You knew you were not the most academic, but this did not stop you.

You confided in some of your family members and dear friends (you know who you are) who helped you prove to your family that you can go to university, and you were determined to get the grades you needed. You appreciated the help neighbours gave you. You used their computer, they proofread and checked assignments, and helped with grammar and spelling.

It was overwhelming thinking of a plan to convince your family you were worthy of the opportunity to study before any marriage proposal. It felt like a race against the clock and you knew you were capable of more.

You felt desperate to try and gain some independence and even said you would consider an introduced marriage once you had studied away from home. But how could you shut your eyes once you had them opened with freedom? When you were at university you agreed to an introduction with a suiter. It only lasted five minutes because the man you met was so traditionally minded and couldn't believe that you didn't live with your parents and wanted a career. This reinforced what you needed to do to build the path to be independent and see the world, outside the confines of a small community.

You know your parents were taking a big chance supporting you to go to university and study away from home. You were the first girl in the small community to do it. It was a bitter pill to swallow knowing that some of your family were extremely proud of you but there was also lots of gossip and judgement about your parents and what you might become.

I am going to tell you right now, it's going to feel like a long journey; doing the unexpected and pushing the boundaries, but trust me you can bring on this change. People can't stand in your way if you don't let them. The fear other people have should not hold you back. Don't be afraid of what people might think! You are made up of really strong stuff. I know because you are me. Listen to your gut, it might feel unbearable to feel like you've disappointed anyone, but you have one life to make it count.

You remember your brother coming home on A-level results day and spending hours on the phone discussing clearing options. You hadn't sought permission but you know he had your back. It was an unspoken agreement that you were finally able to go. University was a breath of fresh air. You met some wonderful lifelong friends who you still adore to this day. No one judged and you weren't looking over your shoulder feeling suffocated.

After university you were even more determined. You wanted to move to London and get a job to stand on your own two feet. You were amazed by your family's support and how far they had come.

Now you are older and find out you are dyslexic, and that your brain does operate a little differently. Fast forward twenty years you joined the police for ten years and policed the streets in Hackney (one of the biggest crime-rated areas of London). Policing was an incredible experience, however, now in the corporate world, you're married to your soul mate with two beautiful children. I must add, your parents accepted your non-Sikh husband (who is white) eventually with open arms. Not everyone in the community did, but that's another letter for another time.

What inspired me was my grandad who arrived in Britain for more opportunities. It was illegal in the 70s for Sikhs to wear turbans on motorcycles in the UK. My grandad campaigned hard and was even imprisoned a few times but eventually led to the law being changed in the UK. That is proof that whatever it is you desire you can do it.

Trust me I am you. You are destined for more than being told how to live your life and being expected to do certain things. I am certainly destined for more than a marriage and children. I fought so hard for it and that fight never leaves me. It will teach me that anything is possible and you will get your happy ever after.

It wasn't an easy ride but the easy journeys are not the most adventurous ones.

You make a difference in the world. You matter, you are the person you wanted to be and have a lot to share with the world.

What helped support me is friendships I could trust, I loved swimming and there is something about being in the water that brings lots of calmness to the body. Get out and walk to clear your head, hot yoga is a must to feel rejuvenated. Find advocates that share your thoughts and feelings chances are you are not the only one feeling this way. Breaking moulds, making part of history, being a leader, and an inspiration. So go, go, girl. Talk to your family about how you feel. Parenting doesn't come with a handbook; everyone is learning as they go.

My advice is if there is something you desire, you can achieve it. Do something you are passionate about as it won't feel like work. Surround yourself with people you can trust, that love you unconditionally, who want you to win in life. These people in your life will encourage you, give you strength and pour into you positively.

What's the goal you're trying to achieve and what steps do you need to take to get there? Write the end goal out on some paper or draw it. What does it look like?

So, you know you've got this, and it will be very uncomfortable to challenge the status quo to get what you desire, but being uncomfortable won't kill you or hurt you physically, so use the desire to push through that feeling.

I will never forget who I am, where I come from and to be kind. I love my heritage and what it is.

Love Param

About Author

Param Kaur-Kingston

Param is a 42-year-old Sikh mother, a wife, sister, daughter, niece, great-aunt and a loyal friend. Param is married to her Walthamstow soul mate and lives in Essex. Param is originally from Suffolk and grew up in a predominantly white community. Her background was one with traditional cultural values and she broke some cultural norms throughout her youth and adulthood. Param is the mother to Amelia and Eashan who are being raised in a dual heritage household.

Param is an experienced communications and engagement Consultant with over 15 years of experience in public relations. She was a police detective in the metropolitan Police Service before resigning and entering the private sector. Param is a passionate feminist and loves traveling the world , discovering new cultures and experiences with her family. Param is a small business owner of @traveloutsidethebox and is finding fun, immersive ways for families to expose cultures to their children a style that allows the whole family to connect around the dinner time.

Param loves to try food from around the world, she loves to cook but doesn't follow recipes or measurements and describes herself as a habitual rule breaker, strong-minded with lots of enthusiasm for life. Param aspires to talk and connect with other courageous women who have a story to share on her upcoming podcast 'What would the neighbours say'. Stay tuned to find out more about the podcast.

This is Param first published book and the first time she shares her story and hopes it helps someone out there who needs this courageous story to not let anything hold them back. Param became the director of her own life, she was the first girl to live away from home and go on to further education, she was the first Sikh girl from her community to become a police officer. This is a positive story that will help you tune your focus like a Jedi.

https://www.instagram.com/traveloutsidethebox_uk/

https://www.traveloutsidethebox.co.uk/

Chapter Nine

To the teen who struggles to feel accepted

By Rachael Beattie

To the teen who struggles to feel accepted,

Before learning can happen, you must believe you have the ability to learn. Sadly, many children with ADHD don't. If they have experienced failures, they can develop a fixed mindset and think, "what's the point? I'll never succeed".

Since the age of five, and being told to go to school, I just didn't want to go. I don't really understand the reasons behind why I didn't want to go to school. But I just knew I didn't want to go. Was it because I didn't understand what they were trying to teach me? Because I didn't know how to connect and make friends? Or was it too overwhelming?

I just knew that I didn't want to go to school. I remember the days where I used to cry and cry and cry to my mam, saying: "I just don't want to go mam".

"But you have to go to school," she replied.

I used to think why do I have to?

My mam used to say: "this is where you have your learning", "this is where you connect and make friends", "this is where you grow and learn."

Another day, at the age of thirteen that I remember vividly. Another day of thinking I've got to get the bus, I've got to be on time, I've got to get dressed. I've got to interact and talk to people.

I just don't want to!

I am still struggling in the classroom not understanding what the teacher has been talking about.

And that's when I'd actually go to school.

I'd been missing a lot of school during that time. Loads and loads of school, because I just didn't like being there.

I still don't know why I didn't want to be there. Yet again, it's probably because I just didn't feel like I fit in anywhere.

I'll take you on a little adventure back to when I was about fourteen years old. I started to drink on the weekends in the park. Then it went into going out at night. Still only fourteen years old!

However, I loved being part of a world where everyone was going out. They were older. They were around nineteen years old and I had become one of them.

I was part of this world where I could be going out, getting in cars with boys, getting dressed up wearing makeup, sneaking out, pretending that I'm sleeping at my friend's house. Instead, I was actually starting to go out with these older people to pubs. I am only fourteen or fifteen years old, but actually, at the time, it unlocked something inside of me.

I would save my dinner money. I wouldn't even eat throughout the week so I could save my money to buy drinks, tabs and bus fare.

I would sell my granny to get myself out on a weekend. It was all I lived for. I lived for the fast weekends, the highs, and the blowout music, the getting dressed up, the sneaking about, the connecting with boys via texts - It was just so exciting.

My brain felt really really happy. Extremely happy.

I was using this alcohol as a confidence boost. This was my thing. It really made me feel like I was unstoppable. I felt like I could dance. I could laugh, I could sing and I could be happy. Different. Happy.

Then at about sixteen years old I started to think, "right that's it!"

I'm not going to school anymore.

So I left school with no GCSEs. I left school thinking I was a failure, that I couldn't do the things that I was told I should be doing at that age.

But I decided that I wanted to be in this grown-up world, so I went and started to be in the adult world of college. So, I took myself to our local college, I knew this would be a start of me building my qualification. Having no GCSE's I started at the lower level of ICT but before I knew it I was moved by my tutor to the advanced studies which has never ever happened to me before! College was the place that really helped me to grow. But I was still living for the weekends, using alcohol to be that boost of confidence.

However, before long that turned into Wednesday night, Thursday night, Friday night, as well as the weekend, and using alcohol to get through the days and focus on something exciting.

What I'm realising now, is that actually my brain needs that excitement to feel happy.

So, what does that mean?

Now at an older age, and being diagnosed with ADHD, I know that my brain needs stimulation to be happy.

I know that stimulation can come in many different forms. Now I'm able to understand more and find the right coping strategies.

Things like going to the gym, for a walk, or a run. These were the things that I used to help recover from my alcohol addiction. It was my new confidence boost.

My alcohol at the time was the thing that I used to let me talk to people, to understand, and really let my brain do its thing. But now, being older, I no longer use alcohol to change my mood.

It's great to be able to say that really. I's such a proud moment.

There were days where all that mattered was alcohol and food, things like sugar and binge eating.

The binge eating was out of control because when you eat chocolate, and sugary things in this way, it hits our brains with dopamine.

My brain, I now know, needs lots of dopamine and serotonin to make me feel happy.

The things that I found really help my confidence and coping are strategies like exercise, along with talking therapies, yoga, walking and cold-water therapy.

Walking the dogs, seeing friends, going for coffee, dancing in the kitchen asking for help. It all helps!

Also being diagnosed with ADHD.

This means I have a neurodivergent brain.

My brain is awesome. My brain is amazing.

My brain works amazingly now, but back when I was twelve years old, I thought I was sick, stupid. That I couldn't do it. I was broken.

But actually, we are unstoppable.

Lots of love.

Rachael

About Author

Rachael Beattie

Rachael is the ADHD Cheerleader, Coach and Author. She helps ADHD entrepreneurs to launch, grow and share their business to the world. She has made it her mission in life to help Neurodivergent people to find their confidence and become successful in showing up in the world truly as themselves. She helps people build their social media confidence by becoming more visible so that they can attract their ideal clients.

https://transformwithrachael.teachable.com/

Rachael Beattie | Facebook

Rachael Beattie - The ADHD Business Cheerleader - YouTube

https://www.instagram.com/rachaelb_theadhdcheerleader/

Chapter Ten

To the teen who is hiding in the background

By Michele Dickerson

To the teen who is hiding in the background, afraid to shine her light,

Oh hey! I see you sitting over there to the side, wanting to climb over the invisible wall you built when you left the house, and jump into the middle of the room with all your friends but you are too scared to make a move that makes you feel so seen and that feels scary. So, you sit.

Deep down you try to convince yourself to embrace the uniqueness of who you are, but your heart skips a beat at the thought of standing out. You just want to blend into the crowd, but there's a fire burning within you—a desire for fun, freedom, and acceptance.

You see others enjoying their lives, online and off, and you can't help but wish you could be like them: confident, happy, and unapologetically themselves. Instead, here you are paralyzed by fear, afraid of being seen, afraid of being judged, afraid of not fitting in and even more fearful of disappointing God.

I see your heart. I know it all too well. We are the same.

You wear a mask of the girl you wish you could be. This mask feels like the only chance at fitting in. You work hard daily, saying yes to all the things to make God happy; to meet everyone's expectations, doing all the things perfectly to earn the approval of God and others. This is how you guard your heart to avoid hurt and rejection.

Our teen years were hard, filled with these insecurities and a constant need for self-protection, both emotionally and physically. You've been told your whole life: "the world is evil, be aware of the bad guys". This is why we hide behind a wall built of fear. If there was a positive to this, it would be your ability to read a room. You have great discernment of the people and environment around you.

You have a pure heart to serve others, you're just so scared it won't measure up. If you don't know this yet, you are also a total romantic at heart, excited to live the fairy-tale life you grew up believing was real. You dream of having the sweet friendships you see on TV, but your life doesn't look like theirs and you certainly don't look like any of them. You don't feel pretty or smart enough to be chosen. I cannot wait for you to finally know how amazing (and enough) your heart is.

Your insecurities inside and out are connected. This goes back to the fifth grade, when you started wearing makeup even though none of your friends were. You didn't wear it because it was cool, but in an attempt to cover up all the imperfections of redness and cysts. You feel ugly on the inside because you feel ugly on the outside, and it's embarrassing. It took an hour to get your hair and make up set in just the right way everyday. You avoid mirrors because they make you want to cry. You find creative ways to excuse yourself from being in pictures, always the first one to jump up and offer to be the one taking them, on the safe side of the camera.

And the braces, well... they didn't help our look.

As your social life grows, you want to attend sleepovers and pool parties with friends, but you're absolutely not going to risk your makeup coming off or your hair getting messed up, so you avoid most social gatherings. Eventually, your skin heals up enough to start venturing out, but you limit your time, and always carry make up with you in your purse just in case there's an emergency touch up needed.

As a hugger, you face a dilemma when you meet someone new to share a hug or handshake. You try to avoid it but when you can't, you go for the hug over the handshake, holding your breath and hoping your makeup doesn't wipe off and blow your cover.

A handshake was equally nerve-wracking. Doctors said the extra skin on your finger (from a door injury in kindergarten) would eventually shrink, but it didn't. So yeah, we don't really shake hands, hold hands or wave.

Sadly, you believe people will judge you as a person based on your physical appearance. You thought if people got too close, they would gasp at all the flaws, physically and emotionally, so you excused yourself from most friendships, guarding your heart from the presumed rejection.

Hence, the wall fear built, keeping people at a distance. A place you feel safe hiding behind.

Behind your smile, you're calculating every move. You become very self-controlled and perfectionism grows. The less you felt good about yourself, the harder you worked to get better, be better, do better and so the crazy cycle went.

It is exhausting work to live in self protection mode and ultimately in the constant fear of disappointing God. Every day you live your life in fear of Heaven's Report Card.

As if it wasn't enough to deal with all the insecurity issues your outward appearance caused, middle school and high school would be crushing to your heart. The Lord knew our guarded heart would need a BFF we could trust, so He called us to friendship with Him. This would be the first time you learned that Jesus could be your faithful friend and not a Judge in the sky.

The season came and our hearts collapsed when our parents announced they would be divorcing. Two years later on our sixteenth birthday, your mom would share the devastating news your Grandma left earth for Heaven. You had just spent the past two days with her in Dallas and doctors said even though cancer had filled her tiny body, she was doing better. That would be the last day for many decades you'd acknowledge your actual birth date, instead choosing to celebrate it the day before which was a good day for both of you.

I never knew a broken heart could break more, but it can. It did.

To escape my hurt, I immersed myself in church programs and working to avoid being home. When I couldn't think where to go, my favorite place to escape to was this tiny prayer chapel built into my church, open 24/7. What a holy hiding place. His love was a healing balm even when I didn't completely understand the fullness of His love and heart yet. He let me rest and hide in Him, our Shelter in the Storm.

Watchful, guarded, cautious and smiling. Everything was fine, year after year, behind the wall fear had built!

High School was a blur, but senior year, we met the boy we'd marry. I was working as a hostess at a local restaurant when I heard the crashing tray of plates. I ran to help, and it was him...the cute bartender/server I had my eye on. He tells people that it was at that moment he knew he wanted to marry me.

He asked me out several times and I said no. I wanted to say yes, but I was shy and introverted. Eventually I said yes to a first date after working a double shift, then five months later to the proposal and three years later, saying yes at the altar.

He was a very confident, 'life of the party' kind of guy - everything I was not. He was the perfect person to bring me out of my hiding place and the perfect person to hide behind. While he had been away from the church for a few years, I had been avoiding a social life, together, we brought each other out to the places we wanted to be all along.

The older you got, the thicker the protective wall grew, as you faced bigger responsibilities in life and in the church. You keep an emotional distance from others, not wanting to talk about what's going on. You don't want people to know something is wrong and risk disqualifying yourself in some way from the world of ministry and friendships.

I'm sure you're wondering if the insecurity and fears went away when you started adulthood and became a wife and mom. Sadly, the answer is no. They actually got worse under the weight of raising up your precious babies and the pressure to guard their hearts whilst still guarding your own.

You'll be excited to know you become a Mom to three boys, one girl and three angel babies you haven't met yet. And yes, your insecurities made you believe the miscarriages were your fault.

Serving in the church, you struggle with the deep responsibility to represent how a Child of God should feel and live her life...full of joy, courage, strength and peace, anxious for nothing. You're so good at cheering for everyone but you!

Even though you strive for perfection, nothing in your world validates it. You don't make straight A's, or have many friends, your nose and ears are still too big, your skin is oily and red, and you wonder if you really are just a 'dumb blonde'.

We've always been the type to make lemonade out of lemons, but there were many days I couldn't keep up with all the lemons. Mom tells people we were born with rose tinted glasses but she didn't realise they were always smudged.

We grew more and more exhausted, trying harder to be better and meet the expectations and needs of everyone else.

I began to feel like a human vending machine. I positioned myself lower and lower on the list of things that needed support or attention. It was more than letting go of lunch dates with friends...it was my quiet time, including time with the Lord.

I was exhausted but felt selfish wishing for a break. I couldn't let myself rest...there was always something to get done.

I convinced myself that God, my BFF, would understand taking a back seat to my ministry and my humans who needed me in real life. Surely the Lord appreciated the fact I was 'doing everything as expected, rightly in service to Him'. If anyone understood my life's hustle, it would be Him, right?

You'll come to find out, the Lord was not okay with my justifying His low number of priority on my list. He was #1 in my heart, but last on my list!

This is where our life turned upside down and right side up in December 2008. It was the beginning of a lot of firsts and a lot lasts. Ever heard of a panic attack? Until it happened, I had not. In His loving kindness, God uses this painful season of physical weakness to get our attention and eventually straighten out our upside down priorities. To begin to take down the wall of fear built, brick by brick.

There were warning flags and I ignored them, until I couldn't anymore. At first, I was sad, then I got mad! Why, when I was working so hard to serve and please others in His Name, am I now completely broken, again?!

The very thing I feared all my life happened: the feeling of disappointing God.

This is the season that your heart officially becomes so painful it is numb. But God, His grace is sufficient and His love a healing balm. Tears became seeds for your encouragement in the ministry. We finally understood the heart of God, His grace, that meets your surrender and trust.

Grace that helps you courageously step outside the wall that fear had built. For some, stepping out of their comfort zone means learning to say yes but for us, it was learning to say no.

We weren't created to be everyone's yes. God is the yes! He is also a shield about you as you embrace His heart for you.

One of the most practical lessons you'll learn on your healing journey is the importance of setting boundaries. Saying "no" is so hard for us. We want to please everyone around us and avoid disappointing God. We definitely say yes way more than we say no. Saying yes seemed easier than dealing with the disappointment of a no.

Setting boundaries is essential to emotional and spiritual growth. It allows you to set your priorities, to guard your heart and mind, in order to be intentional with the most important things - like our relationship with God. Boundaries also create healthier relationships with others and don't allow them to take more than you have to give. I wish we would have learned about this sooner and saved ourselves years of heartache, but this is the journey we have chosen. Now we know.

As you grow in your faith and discover how big God's heart is for you, you'll appreciate you really are more powerful and precious than you realize. You have been given unique gifts, talents, and passions that can be used to make a difference in the world. And while you may feel like an insignificant speck in the grand ocean of things, you are actually an essential part of God's divine plan. The world needs you to courageously shine. But I know this is hard for you to embrace as a truth right now, because you haven't found your mentors, your courage or the heart of God yet! You know yourself too well, and yet not at all! How I wish I could go back and help you grow.

As you enjoy your friendship with Jesus, you learn to trust others, through Him. His perfect love casts out all fear. He is your strength, joy, courage and He is a shield around you! And as you walk with Him, you'll experience a peace that surpasses all understanding. What glorious Grace.

Once you surrender to His heart and allow Him to fully hold yours, you'll have the fairy-tale life you dreamed of. There is freedom and joy in the heart of God and it's the most fun thing ever!

God loves you, sees you, hears you and is near you. God has a plan for you, and it's far more beautiful than you could ever imagine. As you learn to embrace your true identity in Christ and let go of the fear that holds you back, you are a testimony to the grace of God. Your worth is not defined by your appearance or accomplishments. You are God's masterpiece, fearfully and wonderfully made. There is nothing you can do to make Him love you any more or less. His love for you is complete. Girl, God knows the desires of your heart, be patient and let go of the control. Surrender and trust Him. Don't be afraid to step out and shine! You are not going to mess it up! His heart is for you and He's got you!

About Author

Michele Dickerson

Michele Dickerson is a Jesus-lovin', coffee-drinkin', and practical & positive-thinkin' creative soul from Texas who is now living in Sunny South Florida with her husband, four kiddos, and a furry pup named Bella. Online, Michele is known as @MicheleWithAllTheHearts, an Encourager's Encourager and Servant Leader who loves to encourage and uplift others.

A Woman of Faith, Michele has spent most of her life serving the church, including staff positions to volunteering in different ministries to being a part of a successful church plant. She has a passion for Women's Events and loves transforming spaces. She loves to worship and believes that chocolate is one of God's many blessings.

In 2009, Michele started blogging anonymously about her inspiring journey of healing from lifelong insecurity, fear, and anxiety in hopes of encouraging others struggling with similar issues. From this experience, Livin' Where Faith Is was born, an encouragement ministry that seeks to help others overcome perfectionism, fear, and insecurity and instead, live by faith in the grace of God. Livin' Where Faith Is is a place where weary hearts can find rest, shy introverts can connect, and feel seen, heard, and loved. Michele's passion is helping the shy introvert to the exhausted Christian woman who is looking for renewed strength, sisterhood and encouragement in their faith journey.

If you want to join her journey in seeking the Heart of God and find practical resources and upcoming heart hug opportunities, here's where you can find her in the socials:

www.MicheleDickerson.com

WhereFaithIs.com

HeartsFromGod.com

Chapter Eleven

To the teen whose sibling has an invisible disability

By Marta Suchomska

To the teen whose sibling has an invisible disability,

I feel for you. I hear you. I understand you. I also hope you will not make the same mistakes as I did.

Hence the letter.

I am sitting here, a thousand miles away from my sister and for the first time in ages I am thinking of her.

My older sister was born on 8th March, 1985. That day will always be bittersweet. She experienced birth asphyxia which was, to some extent, the reason that twenty-five years later, she was finally diagnosed with emotionally unstable borderline personality. In short, that means that instability is certain.

We still don't know if birth asphyxia was the only reason. I presume that genes play a role as well.

"What a day to be born! You are so lucky! To be born on International Women's Day! Whoa! Such a powerful meaning!" - I imagine this is what people would have said about my sister at her birth had there not been complications.

I try to think she was born on that day for a very specific reason. I still cannot see it, thirty plus years on, but I am more than sure there is a higher reason. Or maybe there isn't? Maybe it was an 'accident'. But doesn't everything happen for a reason in life?

Was that a sign? Was it just pure coincidence to be born on such a day?

You might be wondering what has happened? What went wrong? What is wrong?

Let me take you back to the day she was born.

My mom, eight months pregnant, is heading to a hospital to give birth to her firstborn. Imagine, late 80's in Central Europe. Picture it: everything is grey, sad, boring, stagnant, overruled, strict. There are no emotions on anyone face.

She gets to the hospital. Delivery is dragging on for too long. Way too long. My older sister was born with birth asphyxia. In some cases, babies who experience birth asphyxia may have long-term complications such as brain damage, developmental delays, cerebral palsy, or cognitive impairment. Early intervention with physical, occupational, and speech therapy can help minimise these complications. But in 1985 in Poland no one really cared about this and no one thinks of the lifelong consequences. Was the child born? Yes. Is it alive? Yes. Did the child finally make noise and gain a healthy colour? Yes. What life will that child have after lacking oxygen for such a long-time during delivery? Who cares, surely not the hospital. Back in those days no one would think of arguing with hospital staff. No one was really aware of their own rights.

So, with a child that had four Apgar points when born, my mother gets discharged.

The first few months, inexperienced parents thought my sister was developing at the usual rate.

A year and half later, I was born. Having a second child allowed my parents to notice developmental delays in my sister.

As time went on, my sister started using extremely rich vocabulary, way above her age range's average capabilities.

She could memorise very long texts. She had a great photographic memory.

She started reading books very early.

She started nursery. By then, somehow other kids can sense that she is different. So can parents. So can I, despite being very young.

I actually feel like I always knew something wasn't how it 'should be' with my older sister. Sometimes you just know things. You cannot express nor explain, you just know.

I was very young when I started subconsciously avoiding my sister. I didn't want to spend time with her. I was scared.

The rest of our family didn't see any issues, or more likely, they didn't want to see. She attends schools just like other kids- no one has any concerns. She is admitted to hospitals on various occasions- again, no one has any concerns. No one wants to see. No one wants to admit it.

For over twenty-five years, no one believed us that my sister needed additional support.

For way too many years, not one doctor, or psychiatrist helped my older sister.

From my perspective, that wasn't fair on any of us as a family.

As a child I often thought that my sister liked to 'play the victim'. If your sibling does this, you might think that is just a part of their personality. But it can be way morethan 'just personality'. I have seen multiple times that she actually was a victim: at school, being pointed out, being called names. She was a victim and I didn't protect her when I should have, purely selfishly, because I wanted to protect myself. I didn't want to be pointed out as 'the one who stands up for a weirdo'. I didn't understand the weight of the issue she was carrying. At the time I felt that people were falling for her 'act', and it was extremely frustrating at times. I hated it.

What can you do so you don't feel that it's unfair? Listen and be supportive. I know this can be challenging. But my sister was struggling even more than I was.

All I could see was her 'manipulative' behaviour- towards us and others, despite the fact that she herself was manipulated by people taking advantage.

She should have been taught coping skills to help her manage emotions and prevent manipulative actions. Her disability was causing our family to fall apart, even though it wasn't her fault. Yet, if she had received a diagnosis sooner, we could have learnt about it. We would have known not to react with anger and frustration.

I felt powerless, useless, because I have not done anything to support her. I didn't know what to do. It is now possible to learn so much faster and more easily than it was thirty years ago! So, educate yourself as much as you can. Even if your sibling isn't diagnosed, please, Google topics like this. Mental health related disabilities can be difficult to understand. Learn as much as you can about your sibling's disability, its causes, and how it affects them. This will help you understand their needs, limitations, and strengths better. It will also give you a better idea of how to interact with them. Diagnosis can open doors to additional support and correct education.

I have seen her tendency to risky, violent, impulsive, aggressive behaviour. Getting into violent relationships is NOT normal. As much as I understand that you might be scared of your own sibling while they are aggressive, there is a reason behind it. I wanted to run away so that I didn't have to see it anymore. Yet, I want you to learn my lesson. Instead of running away, try to understand their reasoning and triggers, as hard as it can be. They might not even be aware that their actions aren't fully 'socially acceptable'. Do not make my mistake. Don't hide inside yourself. Instead, help them access resources e.g. therapy or support groups (on or offline). If you can and wish so, offer to accompany them to appointments or meetings. If you feel like, create your own support group too, for families!

I wasn't patient enough to cope with my sister. Now I'm aware that spending time with supportive people can help improve self-esteem and reduce stress- and that could reduce impulsive behaviour. As a child/teen I hated how annoying she was, how many times she was repeating certain sentences, music, and patterns of changing clothes. Patterns of eating only selected food in specific ways. Up to today I will not wear certain types of clothes. I will walk out of the stores when I hear specific bands. I will not eat some foods. I don't want you to end up like me- avoiding things, music, food. I want you to learn to be patient.

Talk to your parents about how you could help. Those conversations are hard at the start and can be full of tears. But it's important to have open and honest communication with them about how you're feeling. Let them know that you want to be involved in your sibling's care and ask for their guidance on how you can support them. As much as it is not your role, as you are a child yourself, having a sibling with disabilities often comes with different rules.

Celebrate your sibling's achievements! Things that are more than obvious for you might be their milestones or lifetime achievements. So, celebrate them, no matter how small! This will build their confidence and show them that you are proud of them.

I wish I'd held her hand, instead of doing everything I could just to be away from her simply because I was scared- because I didn't understand. My parents believed it was better to separate us as much as possible- to a certain extent. We often were sent to totally different summer camps; we were visiting some family members separately. Now I know the reason was to 'protect me'. But in the long run it didn't. I didn't get to know my own sister. I only know her for her actions and reactions. I've never even spoken with her like normal siblings do. In spite of sharing one room for nearly eighteen years, I got to know nothing about who my sister was. I didn't understand her.

I haven't done everything that I could have and I don't want you to make the same mistake. Being a sibling to someone with a disability, especially an invisible disability can be challenging. But I have seen over the years that with patience, understanding, and a willingness to learn, you can build a strong and meaningful relationship with your sibling. I wish for you to find your own strength to do that.

Be there for them and offer your love and support as they navigate their disability. It is hard for them too.

Make sure you fight on your sibling's behalf, so they are seen, heard and understood. So, they receive the care and support they deserve. I kept quiet. Don't be me- speak up!

About Author

Marta Suchomska

Marta's journey to the UK from her home country in June 2010 was not without its challenges. Despite her initial lack of confidence in speaking English, she proved her ability to adapt and thrive in her new environment. Marta's entrepreneurial spirit and determination allowed her help female business owners by providing back end, techy HOW TO knowledge about emails, courses, memberships, and more.

She believes in better, not just for herself but also for those she supports, including spreading awareness about phenomenal women in business through her online magazine, Thriving Women in Business. As a woman, Marta embodies traits of stubbornness, confidence, independence, and protectiveness. She is not afraid to take on challenges and turn them into possibilities.

Marta's story is one of resilience, determination, and empowerment. She has overcome language barriers, navigated the world of entrepreneurship, and prioritized her role as a mother. Marta is an inspiration to those around her, and her unwavering commitment to creating a better future for herself and others is commendable. Privately Marta is "forever engaged" and a mother of two boys. Marta is a constant explorer, always striving to provide the best for her little Polish-English family.

http://smarta.newzenler.com

facebook.com/SuchMartaD

http://instagram.com/such_marta/

linkedin.com/in/suchmarta/

http://youtube.com/@such_marta

Chapter Twelve

To the teen who doesn't feel like they belong

by Cassie Swift

To the teen who doesn't feel like they belong,

Do you ever feel like you don't fit in? Do you often feel left out? Do you question why you aren't like everybody else? You do? Well let me begin by telling you that you are not alone. I know you feel it and I know me saying that is zero help, but everyone at some point feels this way, even the 'popular' kids have insecurities, right?

So, being overweight you were always going to be the easy target. Being brought up like an only child (I had older siblings but there was a large age gap and they had both left home.) With a mum who was overprotective, (through love of course,) was going to make you quieter, less outgoing and shy. These things mixed together are not a great combination. But I don't need to tell you that, do I?

You always preferred playing by yourself and found talking to teachers and adults much easier than other children. Making friends was hard from the start. You didn't realise it but from a young age you would change and adapt who you were to fit in, to feel like one of the group but deep down there was always that overwhelming feeling of loneliness and knowing you didn't belong. An awful feeling that I wouldn't wish upon anyone!

In primary school you only really had one friend who accepted you for who you were and I can tell you that you remained friends into your adulthood too!

The transition to Year 7 was awful from the start, you didn't get offered a school. Your mum had to appeal as to why you should get a place in a local school as opposed to one that was a forty-minute bus ride away. You only found out that you had finally won a place at the school less than a week before school began in September. This, of course, meant you had no idea where you were going, you hadn't met your form tutor or anyone else in your form and with only a couple of people who you didn't talk to going from primary school, you knew no one.

To say you were worried, scared, frightened and actually absolutely terrified on that first day in high school is an understatement. I remember so vividly as I write to the eleven-year-old me, who I feel so sad for, no one had a clue how you felt. You were already very good at wearing masks. Sitting in that hall, with no clue who your form tutor was, having to be taken to your class after everyone else to be introduced, the discomfort I feel now just thinking about it! The awkwardness, the deathly silence as you walked in and were introduced and had to find somewhere to sit, wishing the ground would just open up and help you disappear at that very second.

The funny looks, the whispering, the giggling and being ignored everyday was a living torture. You would do anything to get out of going out at break and lunch and being the 'sad loner,' the 'weirdo', 'the nun' with the ankle length skirt, even if that did open you up to a whole new topic of ridicule. Obviously offering to stay in and help the teacher meant you were an 'a*** licker', a 'teacher's pet', a 'saddo', but somehow that was better than going out and seeing everyone else fitting in somewhere. It wasn't as painful.

P.E. was another place that just felt like torture and you would do anything to escape the public humiliation. Of course being overweight and a loner meant that no one ever picked you for anything. You knew that you would be last and to make it worse, whatever team did get stuck with you would loudly complain whilst others laughed. There was a screaming agonising pain inside of you that you dare not share with anyone. Why didn't people like me, why didn't they give me a chance, why couldn't I just be like everyone else?

When you had to go out, the wall by the school office became your go to place. It wasn't exactly hidden but it was as close to that as you could get, and you would read. How you loved to read and still do, the escape from reality that books gave you was a sense of security in a strange way. Of course people ridiculed you, but they were going to whatever you did, so did it really matter? At least you were doing something you enjoyed.

This was pretty much your life for the best part of 2 years. Laura was the first person to talk to you and make an effort but you felt too awkward and didn't really know what to say. Was she going to just trick you and then make fun of you? Distrust and scepticism were very much at the front of your mind. The need to protect yourself from anymore embarrassment was your main objective now. The anxiety you felt every single day getting stronger but having to hide it because school wasn't a choice. It had to be done, so keeping your head down and getting on with it was what I did, longing for that last bell of the day to go.

After a few times of asking you took Laura up on her offer to 'hang out' although the dislike on others' faces was clear to see. You did try to fit in and laugh at the right places and say the right things but it was exhausting, constantly acting like someone else and even then not really fitting in or being accepted.

In Year 9 after the death of a fellow classmate things did change slightly, the meanness not quite as bad. Allowing you to hang out but not being acknowledged was hard, but it was a step forward right?

Around this time the school started a Christian Union which you went to but again this gave the others ammunition on a plate. You tried so hard to hide you were going even though you did enjoy it and actually began to think that maybe you did fit in somewhere. But when others discovered where you were going you were a 'Bible basher', a 'Jesus creeper', and of course it meant you would try to make everyone a Christian! Why did it all have to be so difficult? Everyone always says: "enjoy school, they are the best years of your life". What a load of rubbish, it was like a daily punishment, a punishment for merely existing. A reminder every day that I didn't fit in, that I wasn't likeable unless I acted like someone I wasn't. A reminder that anything I did enjoy was mocked and ridiculed.

Things began to change slightly when I lost weight. People did talk to me more even though it was fake, back then even acknowledging your existence was a massive step forward in your eyes. Now you weren't as fat, you were more likeable. Of course, this is not the truth but back then at the age of fourteen and fifteen, that was the connection. The fact people were now speaking to you made you feel like you belonged somewhere and that you had 'friends' although deep down the emptiness and loneliness was still there. You thought that would change when you had friends and people to hang out with, but it didn't. The only thing that changed was the overwhelming loneliness you now felt even though you were surrounded by people.

You thought that if you spent more time with them things would change, but it didn't, it became even harder! Going to the toilet at break and lunch so they could smoke, hiding in the cubicle when a teacher came in, knowing if you got caught with them you would get into the same trouble. Skipping class was another one - and if you still went to class and was asked about it later, having to lie. All of this uncomfortableness, going against your true beliefs and values, for what, for wanting to be accepted into a group where you felt on your own and isolated. Why did you do it? That longing to be accepted, that longing to feel worthy of friends. The need to feel good enough, that is why!

That is why you continued your teen years never quite fitting in, no matter what you did or didn't do. The only person you could trust was Laura, the very same person who made the effort all those years ago, and I can tell you, you were best friends. She went on to become godmother to your children and would do anything for you. You knew you could trust her and wondered if she felt this way sometimes too!

You spent years looking for something that no one could give you, years of putting other people before you, people pleasing and staying quiet so you didn't upset anyone. The reason things got to this point was because you no longer knew who you were. You had been acting, disguised and hiding for so long that you didn't know who you were. You'd lost yourself trying to fit in with people who only heightened your anxiety.

When in their company laughing and joking out loud but internally, you had never felt so alone.

Because of this it carried on into your adult life never feeling like you belonged, never feeling good enough. This only changed when you learnt to take the mask off. You learnt to find your voice. For you, belonging to a church gave you all the validation you needed: not being scared to say you were a Christian; the love and support you received from people who you had only just met! A deep connection and unexplainable feeling.

This isn't all about religion though, it was realising you as a person are unique there is no one else like you and there never will be. I often say now 'I am uniquely perfect', why? Because everyone's differences and everyone's little quirks make them who they are and being able to show and share these with the world are so important. As it is only when we show our true authentic selves that others can see the beauty that we hold, and then at that point we will find the people who accept us and love us for who we are. They won't attempt to change you or make you feel isolated because they will see you, and I mean truly see you, for who you are!

If people know what they are getting they can make an informed decision. They can accept me for who I am or move on. A bit like Marmite, you either love it or hate it and whilst this won't be easy (in fact it will be really difficult), you will grow in yourself and you will know your worth and if only you had realised this as a teenager it would have saved many years of heartache and disappointment.

So my one bit of advice would be, to be the True You, no exceptions and you will find your tribe, your group of people where you can be yourself and be accepted. Never be embarrassed of who you are, we are all here for a purpose, to fulfil a mission that only we can. It is our uniqueness which will enable us to do this!!

So be you, be true and be uniquely perfect! Shine your light for others to see and the right people will see it and head in your direction!

'You weren't made to fit in, you were born to stand out.
Jim Caviezel

About Author

Cassie Swift

Cassie is a passionate children's mental health advocate and a children's and teens' life coach within her business True You Children's Life Coaching. Cassie is also the founder and organiser of the Children's Mental Health Matters Summit - and also a single mummy to three young, beautiful, caring, and mischievous girls.

As a child herself, Cassie experienced bullying throughout her entire school life, and due to this, she obviously didn't enjoy school. Cassie wishes that there had been a children's life coach available for her to have turned to, because as a result, over the years, her mental health deteriorated. This is not something anyone would wish for a child, and no child deserves to feel this way or experience what she went through.

www.trueyouchildrenslifecoaching.co.uk

https://www.facebook.com/TrueYouChildrensLifeCoaching

Further Support

If you are struggling right now and need further support please speak to a medical professional.

Here are some organisations that can help:

Young Minds: Mental Health Support For Young People | YoungMinds (www.youngminds.org.uk)

Childline: Childline | Childline (www.childline.org.uk)

We Mind and Kelly Matters: We Mind & Kelly Matters (wemindandkellymatters.org.uk)

Acknowledgments

Wow, what a journey this second book collaboration has been!

I am thankful to all the authors for trusting me with their stories and being part of this awesome adventure! To see the authors open up and use their letter writing as a way to help process past experiences has been an real privilege. Their enthusiasm to want to make a positive impact on future generations is amazing and I am thankful to have partnered with them through *Letters to my Teenage Self Volume Two*.

Thank you to my family and friends for all their support in this process and to God for sustaining me through the hard times.

Thank you to Sophie for providing training in epistolary writing, editing and her ongoing encouragement throughout this process. Thank you to Marta for helping with cover design and Lou for accessibility.

Thank you reader for taking the time to read *Letters to my Teenage Self Volume Two,* I hope that it has inspired you and helped you know that you are not alone in your struggles.

Printed in Great Britain
by Amazon

25170198R00086